THE
FAMILY
CREATIVE
WORKSHOP

Beachcombing, Beadwork, Bean-Bags,
Belts and Buckles, Bicycles,
Birds and Birdhouses,
Birthday Celebrations, Block Printing,
Bonsai, Bookbinding,
Bottle Cutting, Bottle Gardens

Plenary Publications International, Inc.

The Project-Evaluation Symbols appearing in the title heading at the beginning of each project have these meanings:

Estimated time to completion for an unskilled adult:

 Hours

 Days

 Weeks

Suggested level of experience:

 Child alone

 Supervised child or family project

 Unskilled adult

 Specialized prior training

Tools and equipment:

 Small hand tools

 Large hand and household tools

 Specialized or powered equipment

Publishers

Plenary Publications International, New York.

Allen Davenport Bragdon, Editor-in-Chief and Publisher of the Family Creative Workshop. President, Plenary Publications International, Inc.

Nancy Jackson, Administrative Asst. Wilson Gathings, Producing Editor. Jackson Hand, Consulting Editor.

Editorial Preparation

Wentwork Press, Incorporated, New York.

Walter Ian Fischman, Director. Jacqueline Heriteau, Editor. Francesca Morris, Executive Editor. Susan Lusk, Art Director. Frank Lusk, Director of Photography.

For this volume

Contributing editors: Francis L. Barton, Ray Gill, Jo Anne Jarrin, Jay Jonas, Lura La Barge, Barry Lewin, Jane Miller, Richard Natale, Connie Reuther, John Savage. Jasmine Taylor, Roy Williams, Sally Foy, Anne Masters.

Contributing illustrators: Leslie Logue, Frank Lusk.

Contributing photographers: Francis L. Barton, Ray Gill, Jackson Hand, J. D. King, Susan Lusk, John L. Morris.

On the cover
Hand-strung bead necklaces of glass, beans, amber, French jet. See the Beadwork entry, beginning on page 16. Photograph by Paul Levin.

ISBN 0 705 4 0331 9

Filmsetting by C. E. Dawkins (Typesetters) Ltd., London, SE1 1UN.
Printed in Holland by Smeets Lithographers, Weert.
Bound by Proost en Brandt N.V., Amsterdam.

Contents

Pictured on this page are four different kinds of beaches. The fine sand beaches between rocky promontories in the U.S. Virgin Islands are home base for tropical amphibious life. Below left: Pemquid Point, Maine, plunges a granite fist out from the cold north-east Atlantic coast. Below centre: Nantucket Island's tidal marshes are protected from the open sea and provide a haven for mid-Atlantic marine life and sea birds. Below right: Lake Welch, in New York State's Harriman Park, provides the quiet coves typical of many freshwater lakes.

BEACHCOMBING

Harvest the Shore

By J. Frederick North

To beachcombers, the lure of the beach is its constant change. Walk near the water on any two mornings in a row and, if your observation is keen, you will see that life has waxed and waned in the shallows and the moist subsurfaces of the sand, that wind and wave have reshaped the shoreline and provided new materials for the collector.

Beaches are busy places. Waves pounding on the shore deposit sand, shells, and pebbles there. They also break up the material they find there and tow some of it back into the water, where strong currents carry it away, eroding the shoreline. New sand is formed as successive waves, acting like a giant tumbling machine, crunch large fragments against one another, breaking them into ever finer pieces. Meanwhile, new supplies of rock fragments and sediment, carried by streams and rivers, come constantly to the shore.

How waves are formed

Waves are almost always creatures of the wind—even though no wind may be blowing at the time. Tides move water, too, but the action of the wind often conceals the water movement of the tide. So you cannot always tell which way the tide is running. The windblown waves may be moving in the opposite direction.

As it travels across the water, the top part of a wave is pushed by the wind and the bottom part is held back by friction, so it moves more slowly than the top part. This produces the rolling effect. As the tiny waves or ripples build up, the wind catches them and makes them increasingly bigger. Thus, the size of waves depends on the strength of the wind and on its duration. For this reason, waves are larger on large bodies of water than on smaller lakes and streams.

Waves that come ashore no more often than six or seven per minute will build up beaches, since the base of the wave (called the swash) deposits sand and other material as it moves across the beach. If waves hit more frequently, the depositing action is interrupted. Storms that produce a more frequent pattern of waves often cause much damage to beaches. Erosion also occurs when waves hit the beach diagonally, moving the sand in the direction of the wave. This destructive process is called longshore drift. Man-made, wall-like constructions running out into the water at right angles to the beach —called groynes—are designed to help to retain the sands when the waves consistently strike the beach at an angle.

The tidal patterns

The rise and fall of tides are caused by the changing gravitational pull of the moon and the sun. Tides are much greater in some areas than in others. In the Bay of Fundy, between Nova Scotia and New Brunswick, tides frequently run 12 to 18 metres between high and low. When the sun and the moon and the earth are lined up, the pulls of moon and sun are combined. The result is spring tides—higher on the high tides and lower on the lows. This comes at the time of a full moon and of a new moon. When the sun and the moon are at right angles (at times of the half-moon), tides run lower at high tide and higher at low tide. These tides are called neap tides.

A high tide comes roughly 12 hours and 25 minutes after the previous high. The low tides come about halfway between. Thus, tide changes occur a little less than an hour later each day than they did on the previous day, due to

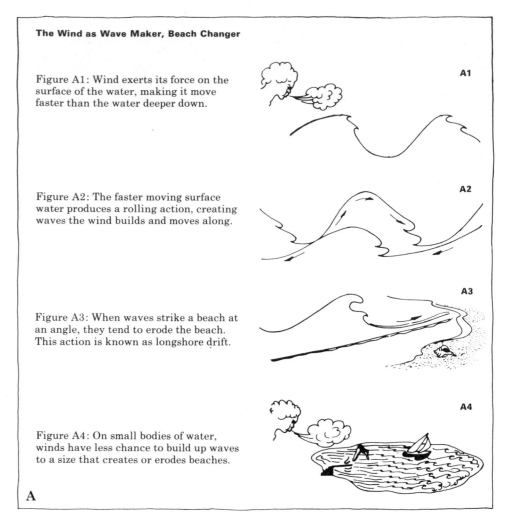

The Wind as Wave Maker, Beach Changer

Figure A1: Wind exerts its force on the surface of the water, making it move faster than the water deeper down.

A1

Figure A2: The faster moving surface water produces a rolling action, creating waves the wind builds and moves along.

A2

Figure A3: When waves strike a beach at an angle, they tend to erode the beach. This action is known as longshore drift.

A3

Figure A4: On small bodies of water, winds have less chance to build up waves to a size that creates or erodes beaches.

A4

A

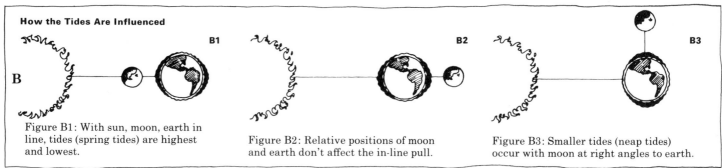

How the Tides Are Influenced

B

Figure B1: With sun, moon, earth in line, tides (spring tides) are highest and lowest.

B1

Figure B2: Relative positions of moon and earth don't affect the in-line pull.

B2

Figure B3: Smaller tides (neap tides) occur with moon at right angles to earth.

B3

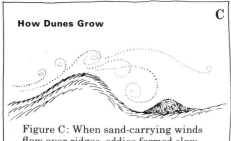

C

How Dunes Grow

Figure C: When sand-carrying winds flow over ridges, eddies formed slow wind down until it drops the sand, building a dune.

the constant change in the relative positions of the earth, sun, and moon.

Only very large lakes have perceptible tides. Estuaries and other outlets to the oceans are affected by tides, and if a river runs into the ocean on a relatively flat plane, it will be tidal for some distance up from its mouth.

How sand dunes are formed

Sand dunes are formed in several ways. Wet sand may capture skating particles of dry sand, which in turn become wet and trap more particles. Also, sand-laden winds travel over hillocks, creating eddies, which whirl down and drop the sand before they spin upwards again. Beach grasses also build dunes by filtering the sand from the winds or by slowing the winds enough to let the sand fall out.

Water lilies are common in still, fresh
water a few feet deep. Their presence
is a promise that you can find a variety
of aquatic life in the mud below.

Not all plant life you will find on
beaches is of the marine variety. On
desert-like beaches, cactus may be found
blooming in the spring or summer.

Water's-edge collectables

Wherever land and water meet, both teem with life. The variety of
collectables is greater along ocean shores than on fresh-water beaches, which
don't have the powerful surfs and tides that flood a beach and then recede,
depositing a treasure-trove of specimens you can collect.

In fresh waters

Although they cannot compare with salt waters in the number and variety of
specimens, fresh waters still abound in natural phenomena for the collector.
The lower forms of life include algae you will find clinging to submerged
stones and driftwood. Since many larger water dwellers feed on algae, you
will find them near by—snails, flatworms, caddis-fly larvae, and others.
Look for hydras, nematodes, midges, and dragonfly larvae. Resting on the
bottom or burrowing in sand or mud are mayflies and their larvae, which
often look like tiny bits of wood. Turtles, crayfish, snails, clams, and other
shellfish can also be found. And don't forget tadpoles and frogs.

Rooted on shore or in shallow water are cat's tails, sweet flag, bur-reed,
arrowhead, and many more species of weeds and flowers—some of them
with blooms more lovely than many land-bound flowers. All are fun to
collect and preserve.

Don't confine your fresh-water beach forays to daylight. Many of the 160
or so species of crayfish, shrimp, clams, mussels, and other shell types are
quite active at night. Sometimes they may be found under overhanging trees
in the shade, particularly on cloudy, overcast days. Quite often, the best
time to find frogs and toads living in swampy places is at night. Follow
their night-time sounds, and use a torch to spot them.

In salt waters

Life began in the sea, it is commonly believed—and that's where much of it
is today. When the tide is low, every square inch of shoreline—sandy, rocky,
weedy, flat or steep—abounds in marine life or the remains of marine life.
Between tide marks you can find everything from a bird called the turnstone
(that is what it does to find its food) to a variety of seaweeds, hard and
soft-shell crabs, clams, fragments of coral, and natural stones—plus shards
of glass so numerous and colourful you can't resist picking them up (for
what to do with them, see the project on page 11).

On the inshore bottom, just below the low mark, there are still more types
of seaweed, frequently harbouring other life. Look closely at rocks, quays,
and wharves for barnacles and starfish. Keep your eyes open for hermit
crabs and oysters. In shallow waters, your eye will discern fish, shrimp,
jellyfish—and sometimes sea anemones.

The sea fans look like plants but are
actually skeletons of many minute
creatures, strung together. Break and
shape them to achieve the effect you
want in your aquarium arrangement.

Nature and Ecology
An Aquarium Tank

This simple tank is ideal for displaying collected specimens. Its dimensions can be changed to fit the shelf space available. To make it, you will need five pieces of 6 mm-thick glass with partially-finished seamed edges. The front, back, and bottom pieces are 25 by 30 cm; the two end pieces 24 by 29 cm. You will also need a tube of aquarium sealer (sold by aquarium-supply stores), a 28 by 33 cm piece of 12 or 15 mm-thick particle board, 1 m 20 of 12 mm-square wood strips, cellulose tape, and a roll of 5 cm-wide, self-sticking, waterproof tape (sold by hardware shops).

To form the frame for the bottom glass, cut two 31.5 cm lengths of the wood strip, to go across front and back, and two 26.5 cm lengths for the ends. Glue these to the chip board base with all-purpose white glue. Strips should butt against each other at the corners. Squeeze a bead of sealer around the inside bottom of the frame formed by the wood strips. Then set bottom glass inside frame. Next, squeeze a bead of sealer around the bottom glass next to the wood-strip frame. Stand front, back, and end pieces of glass in this sealer, securing them temporarily at the corners with small strips of cellulose tape, as in photograph 1. Front and back pieces should overlap end pieces. Now, one by one, separate each corner; apply sealer on edges of glass that will overlap; press corner back together, and re-attach temporary tape. When sealer has set (see instructions on package), remove temporary tape and apply permanent weather-strip tape as in photograph 2. Finally, squeeze a full bead of sealer along all inside joints, and smooth it into a cove shape with your finger. Wait 48 hours before filling tank.

Certain basic rules apply to almost all aquarium life, whether the aquarium is a simple display tank such as this or an elaborately controlled commercial one. It is not wise to mix specimens from different environments. Sharp coral can, for example, injure fish with no coral in their natural habitat. It is best to bring home water from the place you collected your specimens. Whenever you do use tap water with fresh-water fish, let it stand 48 to 72 hours before exchanging it gradually for the water in the aquarium. Allow 4.5 litres of water and 20 square cm of water surface for each 2.5 cm of swimming fish. Other rules on feeding, cleaning, water temperature, hardness, aeration, and the like vary with the number and type of specimens.

Aquarium tank in action. Before adding plants, partially fill the aquarium with water. When you collect plants, leave them attached to the stones or wood they are growing on. Then they will live longer. If you collect live fish from a specific location, it is best to cover the bottom of the aquarium with sand and pebbles taken from the same location.

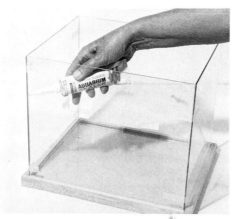

1: With temporary tape strips holding glass sides upright, remove tape from one corner at a time. Apply a bead of sealer where glass surfaces will meet; then re-apply temporary tape to hold glass sides together until the sealer sets.

2: Apply permanent, waterproof tape around the corners from bottom to top of tank, letting it lap over on the inside about 6 mm. Then apply tape around top edge of tank, cutting it so it can be folded over to the inside as shown.

Glass and Plastic
Weathered-Glass Mosaic

By Mark Libby

The best time for beachcombing is at low tide after a spring tide. Right after a storm is also a good time, because the agitated water works things loose and deposits them on the beach. Go off-season or early in the morning, and you will get the pick of whatever has turned up. For beachcombing in rocky areas, wear comfortable shoes with non-slip soles to make climbing over wet rocks and slippery seaweed easier. Plastic or net bags are ideal for

Sail boat on the sea, with sun and gulls in background, in a glass mosaic made from bits of surf-rounded glass.

To make a glass mosaic, you first lay a sheet of glass over your design. Then place fragments in position. As layout for each section is completed, fasten pieces permanently with household glue.

carrying your finds, most of which will be wet. Buckets are good, too. Among my favourite beachcombing crops are translucent, weathered glass fragments. Keep glass separated by colours to avoid having to sort it later. When you get home, rinse your collection in fresh water to rid it of dried salt, which makes it look cloudy.

To make a mosaic such as this one, you will need a pane of glass, worn beach glass of three different colours, some dried seaweed, all-purpose household glue, and 1.5 m of cord.

Wash the pane of glass before you start. Then draw your design on paper or select a picture from a magazine. I sketched a sailing boat for mine. Place the pane of glass over the sketch or picture so you have a pattern to follow. Plan which colours to use for each element of your picture, and work on one section at a time. Place the glass fragments so they abut each other. It's a little like fitting the pieces of a jigsaw puzzle, although the fragments will not fit exactly, of course. When you finish fitting a section, glue the glass in place. Fit and glue each section of the design until you have finished.

Finally, I glued into place tiny bits of seaweed, cut and trimmed to look like gulls in the sky. Let the glue dry overnight.

To hang the mosaic, I drilled holes through the glass, using a tungsten-carbide bit. But you may find it easier to glue the cord around the edge, as a border, and extend it up in a loop for hanging.

claw

walking leg

carapace

tail

tail fin

Figure D: The parts of a lobster shell
that are used to make the lobster-man.

This lobster-man was assembled from discarded lobster shells.
Shellac and a hairy clump of moss finish off this exotic creature.

Nature and Ecology
Make these two from Shells

My cousin Elizabeth made this lobster-man. One night when she was eating
lobster with her family, it occurred to her that she could eat her lobster
and have it too. She asked everyone, when removing the lobster meat, to be
especially careful not to damage any part of the shell. When she began to
work with the shells, she discovered that they smelled fishy, so she soaked
them overnight in a pailful of water into which she had mixed a cupful of
bicarbonate of soda. This not only reduced the odour, but also softened the
shell parts, making them easier to work with. You can still work with them,
however, after they reharden.

Besides the shell, only white glue, common pins, two beads, and clear
shellac for finishing were used to make the creature. The pieces were
assembled as the photograph shows. Start with the carapace, the main part
of the lobster body, and use it for the back. Remove the fins from the tail

(reserving them for the feet). Then fit the tail, upper side out, into the body for the stomach, and glue it in place. The arms, made from a pair of the lobster's walking legs, should be glued on next. Use pins to hold the parts while the glue dries. The joints between the lobster's claws and body make up the legs. These must be even if the lobster-man is to stand, so they will take some fiddling around with. The feet, made of the tail fins, go on after the rest of the creature can balance and stand without them. The head is made of a claw, and the eyes are 12 mm beads.

Assembly-line lobster-men

If you are making several lobster-men at once, you might find an assembly-line procedure practical: Make several bodies; then go on to the arms and other parts. This will allow the glue to dry on one part before you put the next section together. When the glue is dry, remove the pins, and apply a coating of clear shellac. Shellac gives the lobster shells a nice sheen and also helps hold the entire construction together. You might top the lobster-man off with a good head of hair made of a wad of moss.

This sea urchin, when it was alive, had many spines, which helped it gather food.

The beauty of a mixture of miniature shells, starfish, sea urchins, and other marine life is captured in a paperweight made of clear acrylic plastic.

Beach-trophy paperweight

This paperweight embeds shells, starfish, sea urchins, bits of seaweed and grasses in acrylic plastic. To make it, you will need a shallow tin, such as a tuna can, for a mould. You will also need some mould release, clear casting plastic, and a catalyst. Follow instructions for embedding in plastic on page 130. Work on sheets of newspaper in a dust-free place, in a well-ventilated room away from sources of flame. Make sure your sea objects are thoroughly dry and free from sand. Plan the arrangement before you place the specimens on the gel; shifting them around in the plastic is a tricky procedure.

The paperweight is about 8 cm high, so you should begin by pouring two 2 cm layers. Let the first layer gel; then pour the second. Arrange the beach trophies on the plastic, and pour another 2 cm layer of plastic to seal in the objects. If you pour the plastic down a stick, it will feed slowly into the mould and will not displace the beach findings. When this layer has gelled, cover it with another layer. Allow this final layer to cure, and then finish according to acrylic directions.

Lamp was made of driftwood and standard
lamp fittings sold at hardware stores.
The canvas lampshade was bought.

Painting a picture on driftwood is quite simple, especially if you have a talent
for drawing. If you don't, you can trace an appropriate illustration from a book.

Woodworking and Constructions
Make things from Driftwood

The driftwood lamp on this page is one of my projects. The birds on the log
are the creation of Douglas Ertman, an eight-year-old seaside neighbour. His
mother painted the birds on the driftwood plank.

The driftwood lamp requires no special tools except a long 1 cm bit—
or an extension shaft for an ordinary bit you can buy at an ironmongers.
Select a piece of driftwood wide enough at the base so it will not tip when
the weight of lamp parts is added at the top. Let driftwood dry for a
few days—longer if it is deeply soaked. Then use a wire brush to remove sand
and bring out the wood's texture. Make sure one end of the wood is square
and flat to provide a base. Saw it square if necessary.

Fasten the wood in a vice, cushioning it with some padding to avoid
marring it. Drill a 1 cm hole up from the centre of the base and out the top.
Next, drill another hole from the side, 2.5 cm up from the bottom, to meet

the central hole. These holes allow the lamp cord to go up through the base. It will be easier to thread the cord if the sideways hole slants upwards, meeting the central hole at an angle. Sand the driftwood with coarse, then fine sandpaper, and give it a coat or two of clear wood sealer.

To wire the lamp, you need the following: a standard lamp socket, a lampshade support, a piece of threaded tube, about 2 m of lamp cord, a plug for the end of the cord. The threaded tube should be long enough to extend about 12 mm above the lamp base, but not so long that it closes off the hole at the side of the wood.

Thread the lamp cord through the tube. Strip about 12 mm of insulation off the ends of the two wires. Separate the sleeve from the base of the socket and attach the wires to the screws. Reassemble the socket, screwing the sleeve and the base together. Screw the tube into the socket, and tighten setscrew. Guide cord through hole in base of support. Then tie a tuft of cottonwool to one end of about 15 cm of thread; tie other thread end to lamp cord. Guide cotton tuft, thread and cord down into central hole in lamp until it reaches side hole opening. Use suction end of vacuum cleaner to draw cottonwool tuft through side hole; pull on tuft gently until attached cord follows. Insert tube into central hole, and attach wire ends to a plug.

Painted driftwood and birds

Before you start to paint, be sure the driftwood is dry, and sand away any excessive roughness. Work freehand if you have an artistic bent, or trace a picture in a book or magazine. You can use ordinary paint or a special acrylic artist's paints that art shops sell.

For the row of birds, Douglas selected a small driftwood log and dried pods of knotted wrack seaweed. Big pods facing towards the rear formed the bodies. Smaller pods, glued to the bodies so they faced towards the front, made the heads. Doug dabbed on the eyes with black paint. The varying colour of the dried pods made a colourful row of birds.

Sun-bleached driftwood forms a wonderfully neutral base for the assembly of birds made from multicoloured, dried pods of a seaweed called knotted wrack.

You can identify knotted wrack from this photograph. It grows on sheltered, rocky shores, and its air-filled pods act as buoys to keep the plant afloat.

BEADWORK

Bright Accents

By Louise Kropilak

Beads and beadwork have existed since early man hung prized stones, bones, and shells around his neck. Beads were used to decorate fabric almost as soon as fabric was invented. Beadmaking industries were already flourishing in Europe when traders found new markets for manufactured beads in Africa and America. The uniformly-sized seed beads added impetus to American Indian beadwork. Today's native quillwork designs are readily adapted to a lazy-stitch technique favoured by the Sioux tribes, as French floral patterns are to the couching traditionally used by Great Lakes tribes. (Couching in beadwork is using a second thread to sew down an already beaded thread to a piece of fabric.) The geometric patterns typical of early Plains Indian work are today used in wider and wider loom-woven pieces.

Today there is also a renewed interest in beads of all kinds—for jewellery, in macramé, in Indian crafts, for novelties—all part of a great handicraft revival. Beadwork doesn't require the special skills that ceramics or wood carving demand. Original work does require good taste in selecting beads, with an eye for attractive combinations of patterns, colours, and textures. Today there is increasing use of natural and homemade beads. But, just as in weaving, for which most people do not prepare and dye the fibres, beadwork done with manufactured beads still allows plenty of scope for creativity.

Beading can be family fun, too. Stringing large beads on a leather thong may be a child's first craft experience, while the mathematical work of developing original designs in diagonal weaving (see page 22) is a challenge for adults. There is something in beadwork to interest everyone. Even simple beadwork requires patience, but it soon becomes relaxing as you develop dexterity in handling the materials.

Jewellery, Lapidary and Metalwork
Selecting or making Beads

Half the fun of beadwork lies in selecting the beads. Anything you can string is a bead. Craft shops and craft mail-order houses offer manufactured and imported beads in myriad colours and sizes, of glass, ceramic, plastic, wood, unglazed pottery. There are seed, pony, and crow beads, amber beads from Morocco, onyx beads from Mexico. There are round and oval, cylindrical and square hardwood beads in both soft and startling colours. From the wide variety of trade beads that come from Africa to zebrawood ovals, somewhere someone sells what you want. They may be made of tortoise shell, petrified wood, bamboo, or plastic. Most craft-supply mail-order catalogues carefully describe the beads offered, noting shape, material, and size.

You can also make your own beads from seeds, nuts, shells, and other easily collected items in nature's storehouse. Sea shells can be cleaned and drilled. If they are shells you collected yourself, you can remove any animal still present by boiling and working it out carefully with a fork. Thin shells can be punctured with a strong needle or a small awl; thicker ones can be drilled with a thin metal bit. Shells with a tile-like surface will yield more readily to a diamond-point bit you can obtain from a lapidary shop.

This small sampling of necklaces suggests the variety of materials, sizes, shapes, and colours used for beadwork. Included here are amber, glass, wood, and plastic beads.

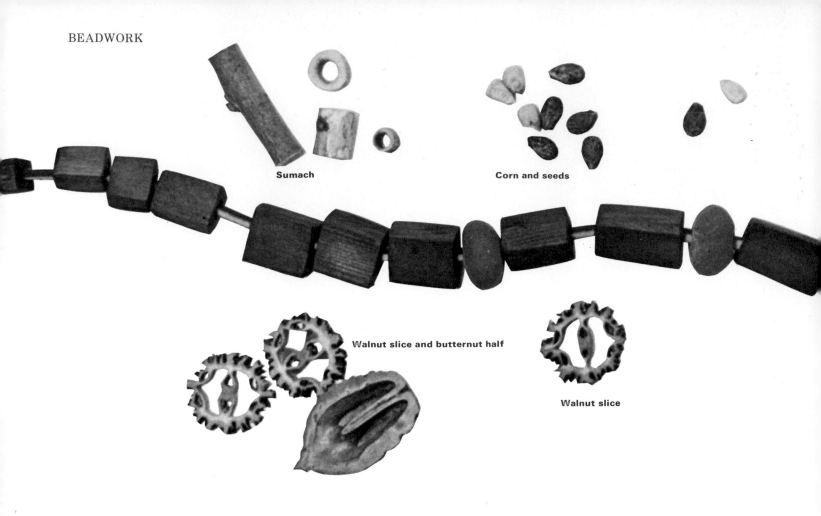

Sumach

Corn and seeds

Walnut slice and butternut half

Walnut slice

▲ You can make beads from many natural things or create some of your own.

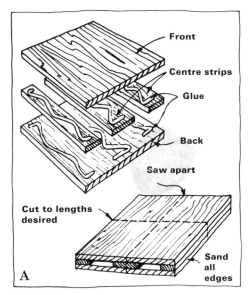

Figure A: To make built-up wooden beads, use a back piece of thin, solid wood. Cut middle-layer strips from wood as thick as holes are to be. Space strips double that distance apart, so two cords can pass through. Add front piece. Glue together, let dry, saw in half lengthways, then cut each block to bead length desired.

Labels in figure A: Front — Centre strips — Glue — Back — Saw apart — Cut to lengths desired — Sand all edges — A

Watermelon seeds, washed and laid in the sun to dry, develop interesting, vari-coloured dark patterns. Pumpkin and sunflower seeds dry to lighter colours. Some seeds, such as pumpkin, take liquid dye reasonably well. After drying, pierce the seeds for stringing and coat them with clear spray enamel, or lacquer. Dried kernels of corn provide a variety of colours without being dyed. You can perforate them for stringing with a strong needle. To cut thin slices of walnut or butternut shells for stringing, use a coping or jeweller's saw with a fine-toothed blade. The nuts' natural oil is finish enough. Stag's horn sumach's fuzzy bark peels off easily from newly cut twigs, leaving a nearly white surface. But if you let such twigs dry, the bark must be scraped off, leaving a grey-brown layer. After poking out the pulpy centre of the sumach twigs, cut to bead length, sand ends, and apply a finish if you wish. Be careful not to confuse Stag's horn sumach with poison sumach, which is as dangerous as poison ivy. The poisonous variety grows in swamps and has downwards-hanging white berries. Stag's horn sumach grows in drier areas and has upright red berries.

If you make beads from a bone, boil it, pick it clean, and dry it. It can then be sawed (with a fine-toothed blade), sanded, waxed, and buffed to a pleasing sheen. Treat horn the same way. You can make flour-and-salt clay beads in your kitchen. Colour the dough with liquid dye or tempera or acrylic paints. Coat any dry beads you dye with clear spray enamel or lacquer, to prevent moisture absorption. Wooden beads can be made as shown in figure A. Wood can be stained and sealed, painted, waxed, or just left natural. Moulding papier-mâché around a straw is another way to make beads. Novelty jewellery may be made of paper clips, safety pins, or innumerable other objects that you might never think of as beads. Aluminium and copper tubing, for example, can be cut to bead lengths and strung. Search your local hardware and stationery shops for such objects. Children enjoy stringing hollow pasta shapes, dried, dyed or painted.

Papier-mâché

Wood

Kitchen dough

Assorted shells

1: If the shell is hard and thick, drill hole for stringing with a hand-held power tool. Always back up the shell with a piece of scrap wood to minimize breakage.

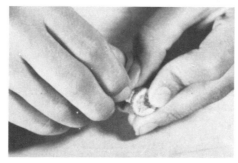

2: Use fingernails to peel fuzzy bark off newly-gathered Stag's horn sumach twigs that have been cut to bead lengths. Peeling produces white, smooth cylinders.

3: Push out the sumach's centre pulp with a plastic knitting needle that has been cut off straight. This will leave a neat, and very smooth hole.

4: To give sumach or built-up wooden beads a smooth surface quickly, use a power sander. But be sure that you finish the work with a fine-grade sanding disc.

5: Mix 100 gm flour with 50 gm of salt to make kitchen clay. Add just enough water to make a stiff dough. To colour, add liquid dye to mixing water.

6: Mould clay around nail or screwdriver. Arrange beads on biscuit sheet, with holes perpendicular. Set in cold oven, bake two hours in a slow oven and turn once.

19

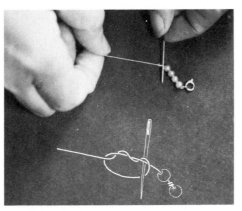

Round and oval wooden beads are used to show various stringing methods: (1) shows parallel threading; (2) is a knotted single strand; (3) is a simple strand; and (4) demonstrates cross threading with two needles. Experiment with relative sizes of beads used for cross and parallel threading to obtain results you want. Make sure that the holes in the beads are large enough to accommodate two strands.

Jewellery, Lapidary and Metalwork
Stringing Beads

A string of beads can be just that, a single strand on which beads are strung. The strand might be a wire, a cord with the end stiffened with wax or glue, a leather thong, or a thread led through the beads with a needle. A knotted strand has a knot between adjacent beads to keep them from rubbing together, and from scattering should the strand break. If you want to string pearls, many jewellers have a repair kit with specially prepared thread already threaded on a needle you can buy. For arranging graduated pearls in sequence, make a simple V-trough of wood or cardboard. Haberdashery counters have sewing hooks and eyes you can use for necklace closures. For large strands, the bead-and-loop fastening shown in photograph 8 will serve. For more elaborate closures, try local craft shops.

Once you have mixed and matched beads on single strands, you might like to try some dual-strand stringing techniques. The first is cross threading (figure B). Practise with a yarn of button twist. Thread each end on a separate needle. Centre an oval bead on the thread. String a round bead on each needle. Then string an oval bead on one needle, and run the other needle through the bead from the opposite direction. For parallel threading (figure C), start with two round beads centred on your practice thread, with a needle on each thread end. Run one needle through large bead, the other needle through that same bead from the same end. Next, run one needle through a small bead, the other needle through another small bead, then both back through one large bead, and so on.

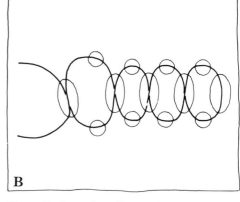

7: The correct knot to use in a knotted strand is a double-twisted overhand knot, run up to position with a pin or needle before the knot is tightened in place.

Figure B: Cross threading works well with round beads at sides of chain, oval beads for crossings. A chain like this formed into a circle becomes a simple bracelet.

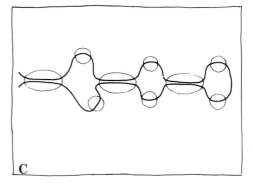

8: From top: Bead and loop, sewing hook and eye make good closures. One-strand spring-lock grip, spring ring with peg, and hook and ring are jewellery supplies.

Figure C: Parallel threading is used for many interesting necklaces. Two strands strung with small beads are run through a large bead, then back through small beads.

Six large blue wooden beads and six grey ones plus 19 small brown beads are used in medallion (right). Brown-and-white trivet (left) requires seven medallions.

Cross-threading a medallion

Once you can do cross-threading, you can make medallions. For the medallion necklace pictured above (right), you will need small needle-nose cutting pliers, a ruler, No. 30 gauge bead wire, 12 large (10 mm) round wooden beads, 19 small (5 mm) beads and 75 cm cord. Put beads in bowl for easier handling and cut a 60 cm length of wire with pliers. Centre one small, one large, one small, and one large bead on one end of wire. Put other end of wire through the last large bead; this completes the first circle, as shown in figure D. Now, on the left wire, string one small and one large bead, and on the right wire, one small, one large, and one small bead. Put right wire through large bead on left wire to complete the second circle, figure D. To complete the medallion, repeat the sequence of the second circle four times, photograph 9 and figure D. To make trivet shown above (left), see instructions on page 22.

9: With three of the four second circle sequences completed, the medallion looks like this. To complete the final circle and the medallion, see figure D.

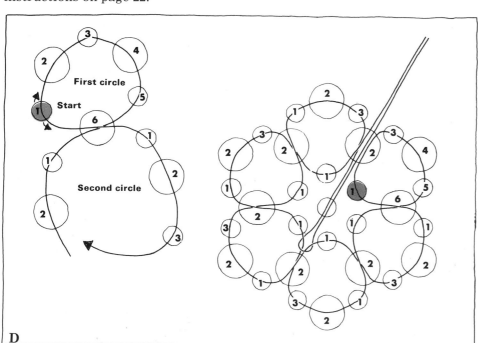

◀ Figure D: How to wire the medallion. Repeat sequence of second circle, as shown at left, four times. Then bring both ends of wires through first large bead. Run end across, loop, and return, adding centre bead as shown at right to complete medallion. Twist wires together, clip short, and bend end into a bead. For the trivet (see instructions on page 22), you will leave the 15 cm ends projecting on the other six medallions.

D

Making a trivet

The trivet shown in colour at the top of page 21 is essentially an assembly of seven medallions. To make it, you will need about 5 m of No. 30 gauge bead wire, 84 large (10 mm) round wooden beads, and 133 small (5 mm) wooden beads. Since this is a trivet designed to hold hot objects, be sure to use wooden or ceramic (not plastic) beads. Use the needle-nose cutting pliers to cut seven pieces of wire, each one 65 cm long. Make the first of the seven medallions you will need for the trivet as indicated in figure D on page 21. This medallion will become the centre medallion in your assembled trivet. The other six medallions are made the same way but with one important difference. After adding the final centre bead and twisting the wires together, leave 15 cm ends of wire projecting, instead of clipping the wires short as you did for the first medallion. You will use these extended wires to attach each of the six medallions to the first (or centre) medallion you made.

Assembling the medallions

When you have completed all seven medallions, place the first one with the clipped-off wires in the centre, then use the projection wires on the other six medallions to attach them to the centre one, as in photograph 10. To complete the trivet, use 10 cm sections of wire to attach outer medallions firmly on to each other.

10: Put first medallion in centre; hook on other six, twisting extended wires to attach each. Cut 10 cm wires to join outer ring of medallions together.

Diagonal weaving

The parallel threading technique (see page 20) enables you to do diagonal weaving. The most successful diagonal-weaving projects are those using straight-sided tile beads, because the rows tend to stay aligned. This form of non-loom weaving can be worked with thread or wire. Small motifs can be appliquéd to fabric; strap designs make bracelets and belts; larger pieces are used for bags or purses. Plotting the designs is similar to graphing for loom-woven beadwork described in American Indian Crafts, *Acrylics* . . . volume. It's a good idea to work out the design you plan to use on special brick-style graph paper, which is sold in craft shops. Or use two squares on regular graph paper to represent each bead.

Making the sample

Making the 8 by 4 cm sample shown in photograph 11 requires 78 small brown ceramic tile beads, 33 white ones, and 2 m of No. 28 gauge bead wire. You will need the small needle-nose pliers, too. Mark the centre of the wire, shown by double-ended arrow in figure E. String 17 brown beads on wire's left end, one brown bead on right. Run right wire through bead 2; add bead 19; run end through bead 4; add bead 20; and so on, following figure E. Turn both wires, as shown, at end of row. To finish, twist wires together; thread back through one or two beads; clip ends short.

11: Sample piece of diagonal bead weaving illustrates typical design motif, may be used to decorate anything suitable. To make it, follow pattern shown in figure E.

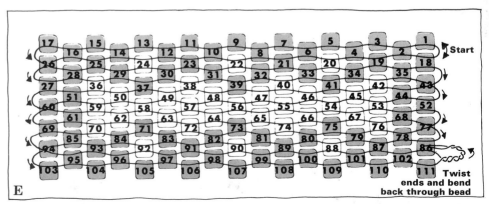

Figure E: Diagonal-weaving diagram for making the sample piece shown in photograph 11. The tinted squares represent brown beads. The numbers refer to sequence in which beads are added. Double arrow marks wire's centre. Step-by-step instructions for making the decorative sample are given in the text above.

Jewellery, Lapidary and Metalwork
Beaded Breechcloth

There are several ways to decorate fabric with beads. One of the most common is to sew on a woven-beadwork strip like that on the breechcloth my neighbour William Spangenberg is wearing over a leather waist thong. Seed beads make the strip, which is about 20.5 cm long and just under 2.5 cm wide. The breechcloth, made for a small boy, is of brown felt 23 by about 127 cm.

To loom-weave beads, see the Craftnotes in American Indian Crafts, *Acrylics . . .* volume. To duplicate this strip, follow pattern grid in figure F. Each square represents a single bead. Warp loom for 11 beads (12 lengthways threads). You will need a bead needle, a spool of white cotton or linen bead thread, and three or four tubes of seed beads in white and mixed colours.

Breechcloth drapes in front, goes over waist thong, between legs, up over thong in back. Duplicate beaded strip on back.

F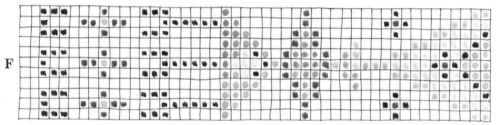

Figure F: Left half of pattern is shown. Reverse on centre row for the right half.

BEADWORK CRAFTNOTES

The simplest way to attach beads to fabric is to sew them on one at a time. Even quicker is to string five or six beads, then take a stitch through fabric. Or work with two threads—one to string beads, one to sew them down. Woven beadwork is tacked to fabric like any appliqué.

Single Stitch: To attach beads to cloth working the single stitch, thread needle and knot thread. Bring needle from back to front of fabric, through one bead and back through fabric—one stitch for each bead. This leaves a space between beads.

Single stitch

Lazy Stitch: This, still a single-thread method, goes a bit faster, gives a ridged appearance resembling Indian quillwork. Thread needle; knot thread; bring needle from back to front of fabric. Thread five or six beads; take stitch at right angle to bead row.

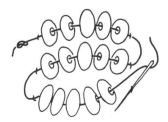
Lazy stitch

Couching: Intricate curves of floral designs, both Indian and European, are executed in couching stitch, with two threaded needles. Thread beads with one needle; position strand on fabric; with second needle and thread take tiny stitches over beaded thread, working carefully between beads so the stitches are invisible. Couching permits solid beading, as no space is left between beads.

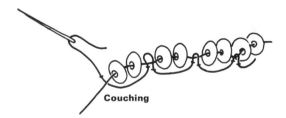
Couching

Tacking: Woven beadwork is tacked on to fabric. Turn ends of woven strip under, and sew or glue to reverse side. Lay strip in position. Knot tacking thread on reverse side of fabric. Bring needle up through fabric between two rows of beads, over outside warp thread, back through fabric. Do not draw thread so tightly that strip puckers.

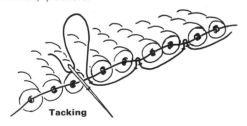
Tacking

Jewellery, Lapidary and Metalwork
Beaded Fruit

By Sarah Muken

There are many ways to use beads without stringing them. They can be fastened to fabric for fashion accessories. Or glued decoratively on boxes and jar lids. That's why some beads are made without holes. Another method is to pin beads into a solid form. Such forms come in various shapes, from flocked animals children can stud with pinned-on beads, to decorative fruit shapes such as the strawberries in photograph 12. When fully beaded, these strawberry forms will look like the glistening berries in the arrangement pictured opposite.

The strawberry shapes are made of a soft plastic specially prepared for beadwork, and usually coated with flocking. To convert them into beaded fruit, you'll need the materials shown in photograph 12. Faceted plastic beads like these are less expensive and longer lasting than most imported glass beads. The large-headed pins are sold specifically for beading. Beads, pins, various fruit forms, and leaves are all available in kits. If you don't like plastic leaves, you could use starched fabric or felt, stiffened by applying glue or paste to the back.

This type of beadwork has other possibilities. You might mount a print on a block of plastic foam and surround it with a pinned-on bead design. Or put a pin through a small seed bead, then through a sequin for a different effect. Pin rows of beads and sequins around the border of the print, as a colourful frame. Or pin beads around a small mirror mounted on plastic foam or some other material pins can penetrate.

12: For strawberry trio, get a bag of 6 mm, faceted red plastic beads, extra-large-headed No. 14 bead pins, leaves, and strawberry forms. Pin first bead into stem end; set next six beads around first one. Continue successive circles to cover berry.

Select a suitable container to display
beaded fruit to advantage. All pieces
are made in the same manner. Concentric
circles around first bead work out best.

Jewellery, Lapidary and Metalwork
Safety-Pin Necklace

With the addition of brightly coloured beads, even the lowly safety pin can become the basis for costume jewellery, like the necklace pictured below. (A shorter version becomes a bracelet.) This is a good project for children. Show them first how three red or blue beads go on each pin (figure G), then how one joiner pin holds six beaded ones together. Make sure the children understand that all beaded pins should point in the same direction, for a neat look. Lay out pins as in figure G. Run the point of the first joiner pin alternately through a head of a red-beaded pin, then a tail of a blue-beaded pin and so on. Next joiner pin goes through with the heads of a second set of blue-beaded pins alternating with the tails of the first set of red-beaded pins. Continue until bracelet or necklace is the length you wish. The fastener is, of course, another pin.

Most safety pins are too large for standard seed beads but will easily hold three E-beads. Vary the colour and shape of the beads, and try silver- and gold-coloured pins from haberdashers or fancy-coloured pins from a craft shop. For a key tag a child can make, put six beads on each of seven fairly large pins. String the tops of the six beaded pins on an even larger safety pin, and run a second large pin through the bottoms of the beaded string, to form a rectangle. Hang one more pin from a corner for the key. Children could also experiment with big beads and paper clips or notebook rings.

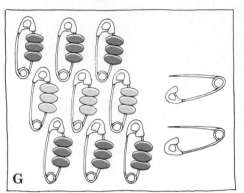

Figure G: Lay out beaded pins, heads pointing the same way. Top joiner pin goes through heads of middle set, tails of upper set. Second joiner pin links middle set with lower set, and so on.

▼ Choker-length necklace uses 104 safety pins, 117 red beads, and 117 blue beads.

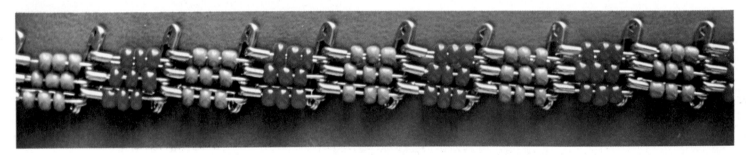

Jewellery, Lapidary and Metalwork
Aurora-Borealis Ring

Plastic beads are available in many styles. Often they are made to look like more traditional beads, but of less expensive and lighter-weight materials. For instance, the transparent beads used for the strawberries (page 25) look like the steel-cut faceted glass beads long a favourite in Europe. Beads of opaque plastic, such as the E-beads used for the safety-pin necklace above, simulate ceramic bead shapes it is no longer economically feasible to manufacture. Other plastic beads copy natural materials now hard to find or too expensive to process, like coral and pearls. The ear drops pictured on page 28 are made with plastic pearls.

Some manufacturers, having realized the unique possibilities of plastic as a material for beads, have produced lightweight, oddly-shaped beads that do not look like any beads ever made before. A visit to your local bead supplier will acquaint you with what is available and may give you ideas for adapting the methods described here and on pages 28 and 29.

The ring pictured on the opposite page could be made of pearlized spangles, worked in the same manner as the rondelles used, and with the same jewellery findings. To make the ring, follow the directions given with photographs 13 to 17. When you see how simply the face of this ring fastens to the ring back (photograph 17), you will understand how to make a set of matching earrings and a pendant drop. You need only select the proper materials. Making a brooch is even easier.

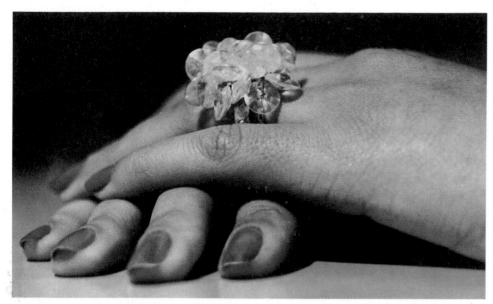

Iridescent faceted plastic beads are canted at an angle by wiring each through its off-centre hole on to the perforated dome. This gives the ring a bulky look with little weight.

13: Materials used for the ring are 14 to 18 aurora-borealis rondelles (which have off-centre holes), spool of No. 28 silver-coloured bead wire, adjustable ring back, and perforated dome finding to fit back of the ring.

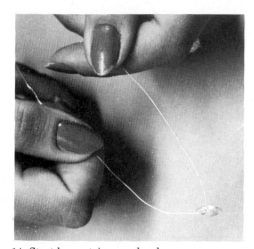

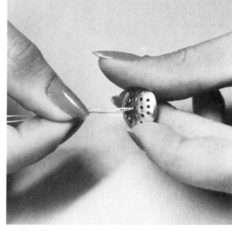

14: Start by centring one bead on a length of wire about 35 cm long. A pair of 10 cm needle-nose pliers with side cutter is a useful tool for cutting, holding or straightening wire.

15: Holding two ends of wire together, push both through same hole in centre of metal dome. Bring ends through evenly, so bead stands partially upright. Bend wires in opposite directions at back.

16: Bring one end up through adjacent hole. Thread on a bead, and run wire down through the same hole to back of dome. Do same with other end of wire. Continue, threading one bead at a time.

17: When dome is covered with beads, twist ends of wire together; clip off excess, and turn up into dome. Secure dome on ring back, by bending ring back prongs up over edge of dome.

Seven groups of simulated pearls, strung on a nearly invisible nylon bead line and assembled with standard jewellery materials, form this attractive drop earring.

Figure H: Centre tiny pearl on 50-cm line. Put both ends through a 8-mm pearl, then through 16 tiny pearls, as shown. Duplicate three more times with each end of line, for a total of seven groups.

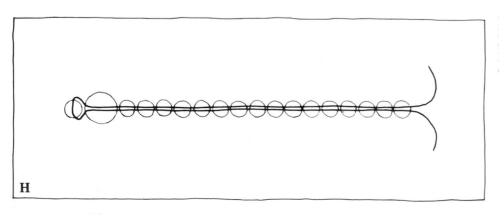

H

Jewellery, Lapidary and Metalwork
Pearl Ear-rings

For each pair of these ear drops, you will need two simulated pearls of 6 mm size, fourteen of 8 mm size, and 238 of 2.5 mm size. You will also need two bead caps, two 5 cm-long eye pins, a pair of ear clips, and 51 cm of fine nylon bead line. The line is similar to transparent monofilament fishing line but much finer. Centre one of the smallest pearls on the 50-cm bead line. Next run both ends of the line through one of the largest 6 mm pearls, then through sixteen of the smallest pearls. You will now have the sequence for one string of the ear drop shown in figure H on the opposite page. Repeat the sequence with each end of the bead line until you have the seven strings forming one drop cluster, as in photograph 18. Knot or fuse ends of bead line holding the pearls.

Now put one of the two 5 mm pearls and a bead cap on an eye pin, as in photograph 19, and loop cluster pearls over eye pin as shown. Make sure that the outside or closed end of the bead cap faces the head of the pin. Make a loop in the eye pin to hold pearl strings in place, as in photograph 20. Close loop tightly, clip excess off eye pin, and attach split ring of ear clip to loop of eye pin as in photograph 21. Repeat for the second ear drop.

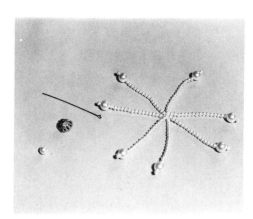

18: Each ear drop is made up of one 6-mm simulated pearl, a bead cap, an eye pin seven strands of pearls (each strung as shown in figure H), and one ear clip (see photograph 21).

19: On eye pin, put one 6-mm pearl and bead cap. Outside of bead cap faces eye. Knot and glue or fuse ends of nylon line holding pearls. Place the cluster of pearls over the eye pin as shown.

20: Form eye pin into loop, to retain pearls. Bead cap is flexible enough to be bent back carefully while you use small pliers to make loop and close it very tightly. Clip the excess off the eye pin.

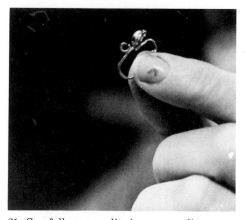

21: Carefully open split ring on ear clip with your pliers. Hook loop of eye pin through it, and close ring neatly, allowing ear drop to dangle freely. The other ear-ring is made the same way.

BEAN-BAGS

Games and Furniture

By Kay Russell Briand

Part of the unique appeal of a bean-bag toy is that it makes a nice melody as it flies through the air and a fine scrunchy noise when it is caught. Even adults seem to be irresistibly drawn to handling bean-bags, and at least part of the fascination of bean-bag furniture is the fun of scrunching around on the bag until its infinitely mouldable filling has assumed the shape you find most comfortable.

Bean-bags as toys have been fascinating children for a long time. The bean-bag is a cousin to, and perhaps precursor of, the ball, which first appears in recorded history in Egypt around 1400 B.C. The ball was made of painted wood, clay, or leather and stuffed with papyrus, hair, feathers, or seeds. Because of the perishable nature of the materials used, little evidence remains of early bean-bags, but a forerunner of the bean-bag we know today is pictured in a sixteenth-century painting. In 1560, Peter Breughel, a Flemish artist whose trademark was canvases crowded with dozens, sometimes hundreds, of people engaged in various activities, painted a scene of children involved in some 80 forms of play. Among these vignettes is one showing two little girls playing with inflated bladders filled with beans.

Bean-bag game

From a simple toss toy, the bean-bag became part of a game that was popular in the past century. The simplest form of the game consists of tossing bags at a board, much like the one on page 35, that has round holes, each numbered with a score. The board is either braced as shown or tilted against a wall. Highest score in a round of ten or 20 throws wins. Another variation on the bean-bag game is Chuck-a-Luck. In this version, the toss board is canvas stretched on a triangular frame. Bags are thrown at numbered, netted pockets. Present-day bean-bag game boards often are in shape of a clown holding colourful balloons. The balloons have holes marked with scores in their centres, and players toss their bags at these openings.

Making simple bean-bags is a welcome rainy-day activity for young children. For the more adept, bean-bag toys and paperweights, like those on pages 33 and 34, have a lot of appeal. Bean-bag furniture, stuffed with plastic pellets instead of beans, is the ultimate application of the bean-bag principle. Mix-and-match pieces like those in the project beginning on page 36 are comfortable, attractive, and relatively inexpensive.

Tools and materials

The projects that follow—basic bean-bags, paperweights, and furniture—are made with easy-to-come-by materials and tools. Most often used are needles, pins, thread, scissors, ruler, all-purpose white glue, ballpoint pen or soft lead pencil, felt marking pen, masking tape, wrapping paper, tracing paper, carbon paper, map pins, heavy-duty cotton, felt, plush, or vinyl fabrics, and a large funnel for pouring the filler into the completed bag. Other tools and special materials required are listed with each project.

Materials you can use for stuffing include dried beans (expensive unless you grow and dry them), rice, cat sand or litter, and polystyrene pellets.

Tossed bean-bag comes in for a soft landing, a quality that makes it ideal for indoor and outdoor use. Instructions for making such a basic bag are on page 32.

Toys and Games
Bean-Bag Toss Toy

Bean-bags can be any shape or size and as simply or as intricately designed and decorated as you choose to make them. The fabrics can be glamorous or homely. Even the toe of a discarded man's or boy's sock can be filled and sewed to make a serviceable bean-bag. Youngsters seem to like geometric and animal forms the best, but usually find almost any shape entertaining. In selecting fabric for a simple bean-bag, look for bright colours and bold patterns. It adds to the spirit of the game and the pleasure of those watching it to see colourful objects sailing through the air.

The finished size of the basic toss-about bean-bag, shown on page 31, is 15 cm square. You need 18 by 36 cm of fabric for each bag. This allows for a 12 mm seam on all sides, the same seam allowance we will use for each of the bean-bag projects. If you never have sewed before, you may find it helpful to measure 12 mm seam allowance on some scrap fabric. Then stitch the seam, and study it until you have a good visual idea of the spacing. Your memory of the spacing may eliminate the need for constant remeasuring on projects where precision is not essential.

Making the bean-bag

The first step in making the bean-bag is to measure and cut two pieces of fabric 18 cm square. Iron a 12 mm seam against the wrong side of the fabric, as in photograph 1; iron around all four sides. Put the wrong sides of the pieces of fabric together, and insert pins along the seam lines but at right angles to them. Work from bottom to top of the seam allowance; then rotate the fabric, pin the next side, and so on. Always pin this way to keep from gathering the fabric. Now stitch the two pieces together along the crease you pressed, leaving an unstitched opening about an inch wide in the centre of one side. Never leave the opening in a corner; it would be too hard to close neatly. Insert the funnel stem in the opening, and, with a spoon and a bowl of dried beans beside you, fill the bag through the funnel. Sew the opening closed, and you are ready to play.

1: When you press the seams, dampen fabric or use a steam iron, and make firm, straight strokes. Don't twist the iron about; it is the heat that actually does the pressing.

The ladybird bodies and heads are made of alternating yellow and red felt. Pieces cut from black felt form the legs, stripes, dots, and antennae.

Toys and Games
Ladybird Paperweights

To make the ladybird bean-bags, you will need two 23 by 30 cm squares of red felt, two of yellow felt, and one of black. Enlarge figure A patterns. For each ladybird you need two head and two body pieces, four legs, one stripe, two antennae, 16 spots. Cut out patterns; pin to doubled felt; then cut out felt. For spots, trace around a one-penny piece with a coloured felt marking pen; cut out. With all-purpose white glue, attach stripe down centre of body top and rows of five and three equally spaced spots at sides of stripe. Glue X mark on each leg to X mark on the underbody. Glue two antennae to top of head so they curve out from X mark on head. Glue head pieces together along seam, but don't glue the area with no dash line; this leaves an opening for the filler. Glue top part of head to underbody, with body extending over head about 12 mm at maximum overlap. Glue body pieces together along seam, leaving unglued areas with no dash line and between dots on one side for filling. Use funnel to fill with cat sand. Glue opening closed.

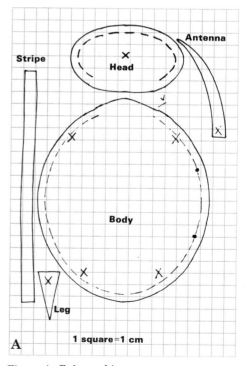

Figure A: Enlarge this pattern, as described on page 129. With carbon paper under the enlarged pattern, transfer it to wrapping paper. Be sure to transfer dash lines, Xs, and dots. Cut out all pieces along solid outlines.

2: Put tiny drops of all-purpose white glue on all felt seams and parts to be attached. Then, with the applicator, spread it over the areas to be glued.

3: Holding the glued-together ladybird upright, as shown, insert funnel stem, and move it about in the body as you fill with cat sand. Glue the slit closed.

33

Toys and Games
Bean-Bag Games

This bean-bag table game is played on a 56 by 90 cm pegboard divided into 25 spaces, each approximately 10 by 16 cm. The frogs shown are made of velvet, five of one colour and five of another colour. For each frog team I used 23 cm of 150-cm velvet. Use grid pattern, figure B, to enlarge frog shape to full size on a piece of tracing paper. Insert carbon between five pieces of wrapping paper and also under the tracing-paper frog pattern. Follow the directions for photograph 4 to transfer this pattern to the wrapping paper. Work on a smooth surface that map pins won't harm. Cut out the patterns; pin them to doubled fabric, and cut out as in photograph 5. Machine stitch top and bottom pieces together on the right side of the fabric, allowing a 12 mm seam. Leave an opening for filling between the dots on the pattern. Using a funnel, fill frogs with beans, rice, or cat sand. Machine stitch opening closed. Sew on matching buttons for the eyes. Tape off the divisions of the game board as indicated in photographs 6 and 7. You will need about 7.50 m of 2 cm black masking tape.

Rules for playing Leapfrog
To play Leapfrog, line up teams in the five spaces at the board ends. In turn, each player moves one space forwards or sideways, or makes one leap over the opponent's frog if his frog is next to it and there is a vacant space to land on. If you leap a frog, you have captured it for your frog pond and can remove it from the board. If one of your frogs reaches the opponent's end of the board, a small ribbon is tied around its leg and it becomes a bullfrog. A bullfrog can reverse direction and also move and leap diagonally, one jump at a time. The player who captures all his opponent's frogs is the winner.

Leapfrog can be played indoors or outdoors. If storage space is a problem, the game board can be made of plywood and hinged in the middle, so it can be folded when not in use.

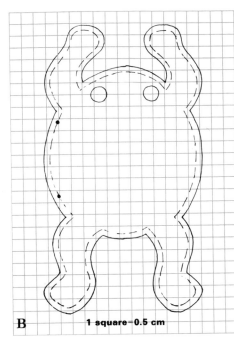

B   **1 square=0.5 cm**

Figure B: Enlarge grid pattern. Follow instructions on page 129.

Richard and Hugh Haas, with their sister Diana playing a friendly game of Leapfrog.

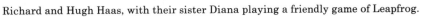

4: With map pins, pin securely through frog-pattern tracing, top carbon, the five sheets of wrapping paper, and the four interleaved sheets of carbon paper. Use ballpoint pen to trace the pattern.

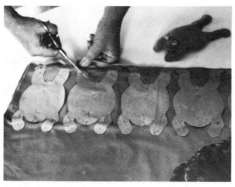

5: After cutting five patterns from wrapping paper, pin to doubled fabric, and cut out an entire team of top and bottom frog pieces. Cut with long, smooth strokes, and hold the fabric firmly.

6: The pegboard holes help you line up the dividing tapes. Count number of holes needed to divide the game board roughly into 10 by 16.5 cm spaces; then stick masking tape to the board as shown.

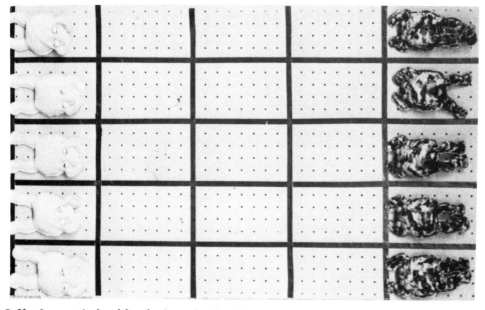

7: Use four vertical and four horizontal strips of 1.3 or 2 cm black masking tape to divide the playing board into 25 spaces. Strips shown on the ends are optional.

To make bean-bag toss board, figure C, you will need one 90 cm square of 10 mm plywood, one 1.3 by 4.8 by 90 cm piece of scrap wood, one 3.8-cm hinge, six 10 mm wood screws, a broom clip, a 4.8 by 5 cm piece of foam rubber, masking tape, drill, fret saw with fine-toothed jigsaw blade, drawing compass, measuring tape, screwdriver, pencil, sandpaper, wood sealer, and paint. Draw a line from centre point of one side of 90 cm plywood square (this will be the base) to centre point of opposite side (this will be the top). Measure and mark 3.8 cm on each side of centreline at the top. Draw lines from each corner of base to marks you made on each side of centreline at the top. Saw along these diagonal lines. Measure and mark centres of five circles, using the distances from the base, top, and centreline shown in figure C. Use compass to draw circles to diameters shown. Drill a hole just inside the perimeter of each circle, large enough to admit fret-saw blade. Clamp board firmly in vice, or support on boxes or sawhorses, and saw out circles. Round off sharp edges at top with fret saw. Make and mount back brace, as in figure C detail, so hinge butts flat against board. Sand edges, seal, and paint. Tape on foam rubber strip. Then add broom clip, bending it open so brace fits tightly.

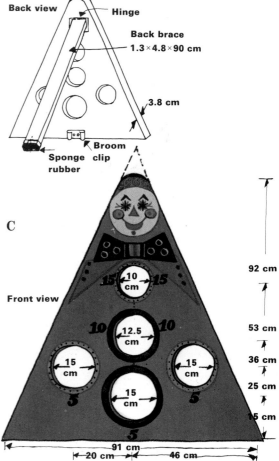

Figure C: Bean-bag toss board may be decorated with clown face and tie, as shown here, or left plain. The bean-bag for this game should be 7.5 cm in diameter and circular. Add 1.3 cm for seam, and make bag as you did the basic one on page 32. Tossing a bean-bag through one of largest circles scores five points. For a toss through the middle circle, score 10 points; for one through top circle, 15 points. Highest score in 10 or 20 throws wins.

Bean-Bag Furniture

Yellow doughnut chair, perfect for daydreaming, and a doughnut hole cushion.

It is surprising how quickly you can cut out and stitch together a soft-environmental creation such as this doughnut chair. The filler of polystyrene pellets is quite soft and compressible, making the doughnut ideal for sitting on, curling around, or even swinging on, as in the photograph opposite. And, as a bonus, the hole from the doughnut makes a tiny cushion.

To make the doughnut and the hole cushion, you will need 2.25 m of 115 cm-wide heavy-duty cotton or canvas fabric, 4 m of braid or fringe, and 1 kilo of polystyrene pellets. For retail outlets carrying the pellets, try your local hardware shop.

Working on a smooth floor or table surface, first fold fabric in half crosswise, wrong sides together. Pin selvedges together. Measure and mark, with a sharp, soft pencil or ballpoint pen, the exact centre of the folded fabric; it should be 57 cm from any fabric edge. From the centre point, measure and mark two points on opposite sides of the centre point, one 9 cm from the centre, the other 12 mm from the edge of the fabric. Now tie the pencil or pen to one end of a 61-cm length of heavy-duty, nonstretch twine. Loop the free end of the twine under the head of a map pin, which you then push firmly into the centre point. Adjust the length of twine until the point of the pencil, held upright, will draw an arc through the marks you made 9 cm from the centre point. Knot twine end under the map pin to fix this distance, and draw the inner circle, as in photograph 8. Next, free the knot, and extend the twine until the pencil will draw an arc through the marks made 12 mm from the edges of the fabric. Re-knot the twine under the map pin to fix this distance, and draw the outer circle, as in photograph 9.

Pin fabric securely around both inner and outer circle lines; then cut out 12 mm outside outer circle and 12 mm outside inner circle. Stitch both circles, leaving a 15 cm opening in large one, for filling. Pin small circles together 12 mm from edge; stitch, leaving a 2.5 cm opening. (Cushion can be sewed with right sides together, with opening left to turn it right side out and for filling.) You may sew braid or fringe to seam edges of the doughnut and cushion now or after they have been stuffed.

The polystyrene pellets make marvellous stuffing because they are soft and lightweight. But they do have a propensity for floating in the air and clinging to clothing. So try to do the stuffing work out of doors or in a

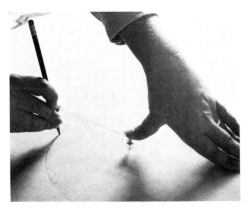

8: Firm thumb pressure is used to hold the map pin very stable. Keep the thumb pressure constant at all times and the string taut. This will help you draw a perfect circle. Make sure circle line is distinct all around.

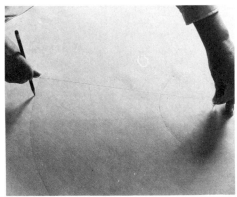

9: In making outer circle, as shown here, you should lift your position enough so that you can continue to keep the string taut and the same constant, firm pressure on the map pin that you used when making the inner circle.

garage or cellar; this makes it easier to clean the working area after you have completed the filling operation. Use a vacuum cleaner to pick up particles.

To fill the doughnut, put the polystyrene pellets into a large plastic bag, which will help confine them. Set the bag inside a large cardboard box, as in photograph 10, so you can control it more easily. Use a large funnel with a wide base and a cup to carry pellets from the bag to the funnel. Because the material weighs so little, you will have to shake it constantly to compress it. Put your hand inside the doughnut from time to time, and press down hard against the pellets to make sure they are being compacted firmly. But remember to keep the opening of the doughnut tightly closed whenever you press or shake the pellets. When the doughnut is firmly packed with filler, stitch the opening closed. Fill the small cushion with polystyrene pellets, and then stitch its opening closed.

10: There is no question about it: it takes two to stuff a doughnut. So don't start this project until you have help handy. Text explains filling procedure.

Richard thinks it is fun to tie a rope around the doughnut, suspend it from a tree limb, and fold himself inside it for a restful and leisurely swing.

Because the cushion coverings are vinyl, they can be used without damage
indoors or out. Clean them with detergent or by wiping them with a damp cloth.

These vinyl cushions, stuffed with polystyrene pellets, make ideal seats
or, when snapped together, emergency beds. Each cushion measures 76 by 76
by 7.5 cm. To make six of them, you need 9.7 m of 140 cm stretch
upholstery vinyl. Measure and cut 12 79-cm squares, starting your measuring
at the top and a side edge of the vinyl. Mark off from the side of the
remaining vinyl six 9 cm strips, and cut each strip the full length of
the vinyl. From these strips you will make the sides, tabs, and piping (the
ornamental ridge along the seams). Using the pattern, figure D, cut 48 tabs
(24 cut double thickness) from the strips. The tabs will be sewed to hold the
eyelets used to snap the cushions together. Using stretch thread, stitch
together tops, sides, and bottoms, with or without piping along seams and
with two tabs 7.5 cm in from each corner on opposite sides of each cushion.
With eyelet pliers, insert eyelets in tabs (circle in figure D). To make zip-
closing covers, follow package directions, but work with tissue paper
between vinyl pieces to keep them from slipping. Paper is torn away after
stitching. Fill and close cushions as you did the doughnut, page 37.

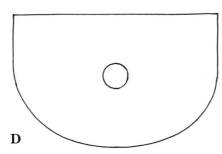

D

Figure D: Actual-size pattern for tabs.

11: Stretch vinyl is tricky to handle, so
practice on a scrap piece. It must be
squared perfectly in order to get an
accurate final measurement and cut.

12: Cushions have enormous versatility.
They can be snapped together to form a
single or double bed for unexpected
guests or placed in a line for tumbling.

Glass and Plastics
Bean-Bag Wall Hanging

Six round bags suspended from a large rectangular bag—all of transparent vinyl—make a novel wall or window hanging. Use the small bags to display little treasures you had packed away, from baby spoons and lockets to valued souvenirs. Materials for this project are available at hardware shops.
You will need 91.5 cm of clear, heavy-duty, 137-cm-wide vinyl; eyelet pliers and eyelets; 1 kilo of rock salt; heavy-duty aluminium foil; four metal curtain rings; a 56-cm length of 1.3-cm dowel; and assorted dried beans, peas, and lentils to mix with the souvenirs.

Cut all pieces of vinyl double thickness. The basic rectangular wall-hanging bag measures 41 by 53 cm. For the round bags to be attached to the basic bag, you will need six 16 cm circles; four 11.5 cm circles, and two 12.5 cm circles. The 5 by 3.8 cm tabs, figure E, are cut as integral parts of each circle pattern. Precise dimensions are not critical; you can trace around saucers, plates, cups, or other firm, round objects that are close to the diameters specified. Use a felt-tip pen to mark the vinyl for cutting. Cut aluminium-foil circles the same size as the vinyl circles; the foil will shield the vinyl from the hot iron. Set the iron to low. Don't use steam. With foil on top of two circle pieces to be joined, work the iron two-thirds of the way around the edge to seal the vinyl; the remaining one-third is the opening into the round bag. Turn the vinyl pair over; place foil on top; iron around edge again, but don't seal the area left unironed before. Repeat process with other round bags. Use a 7.5-cm-wide protective foil strip as you seal edges of rectangular bag; leave opening for putting in the rock salt. Add salt, and seal completely. Insert eyelets in tabs, finished side forwards, following instructions in eyelet package. After placing dried beans, peas, or lentils in round bags, add souvenirs, and finish sealing the bags and tabs. Then snap the tabs to the rectangular bag. Run curtain rings through top of basic bag; insert dowel, and hang the display.

This wall hanging is spectacular when hung in a window or another area where light shines through. Try using it as a novel form of window decoration.

Those little things you like a lot, but have kept tucked away in boxes or closets, can be enjoyed by your friends when they are nestled in a vinyl wall hanging bag.

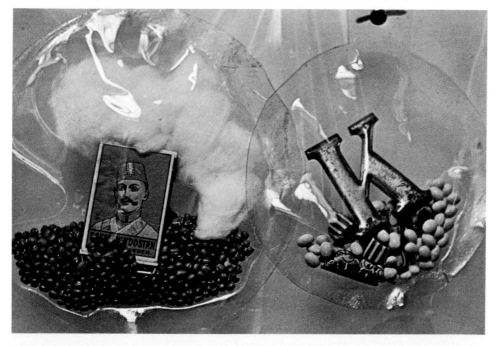

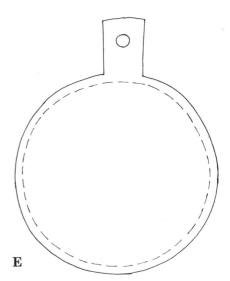

E

Figure E: Position of tab on round bag.

BELTS AND BUCKLES
A Cinch to Make

By David Reppert

The history of belts may not be quite as old as the history of clothing. But we do know, from illustrations on old artifacts, that belts were worn by some of the ancient Assyrians, Cretans, and Egyptians. In the days of the Roman Empire, the girdle (as the belt was known then) became an important part of wearing apparel. It was designed to keep the flowing garments, popular at that time, from restricting the wearer's movements, and it became widely used by Roman matrons and soldiers. The Roman belts had little or no ornamentation. By contrast, the belts worn later by the Franks and Burgundians were often embossed with bronze or silver and had chased or inlaid buckles of superb and intricate design.

In the late part of the 13th century, when the Crusades were in full swing, the crusading knights set what may have been a new record for using belts. They wore two at a time. One was a narrow cord around the waist to contain the cloth outer garment. The other was a wide, heavy belt, slung across the hips to which the knight secured his heavy sword.

By the latter half of the 14th century, belts worn over the hips, swagger style, had reached a peak of extravagant ornamentation. The entire belt might be covered with decorations, and its ornate clasps or buckles often revealed the wearer's station in life, his occupation, and even his religious beliefs. Later, men hung writing instruments, ledgers and other working tools from their belts, as symbols of their trade—and so they would have them handy. By the 16th century, styles had changed and a man's belt became a utilitarian strap around the waist, frequently concealed by outer garments. Then, as loose outer apparel gave way to trousers, the man's belt assumed, of course, its primary task of holding them up.

Tools

Needle and thread: A large, pointed leather needle and a supply of heavy-duty waxed nylon thread.

Cutting and measuring tools: Stanley knife, cobbler's knife, steel straightedge ruler. All can be bought at a hardware shop.

Leather-crafting tools: Circular punch, No. 2 edger, four-pronged thonging chisel, hide mallet, rivets and rivet setter. All are sold by leather crafters. A ball-peen hammer can be used in place of the mallet.

Dyes: Dark-brown and light-brown antique paste dyes, light-brown or dark-brown liquid dye, and a finishing lacquer. These also can be purchased at a leather supply shop.

Tooling instruments: There are many specific tooling instruments, all available at a leather supply shop. However, a swivel knife is a good all-purpose tooling instrument that can be purchased at a hardware shop.

Miscellaneous: Among the household objects needed for making the leather belt are pencil, sponge, dish of water, rubber gloves, matches, and two or three dyeing rags that can be of any material. For buffing the leather belts, a towel or jersey rag will work well.

Durable and handsome, this cowboy belt is a real conversation piece because of the authentic Navajo symbols emblazoned on it. For directions, see page 42.

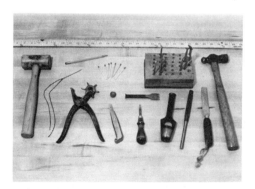

1: Some tools needed for making a belt are: steel straightedge ruler, hide mallet, leather needle, heavy-duty waxed nylon thread, circular punch, replaceable-blade knife, cobbler's knife, No. 2 edger, four-pronged thonging chisel, swivel knife, tooling instruments and ball-peen hammer.

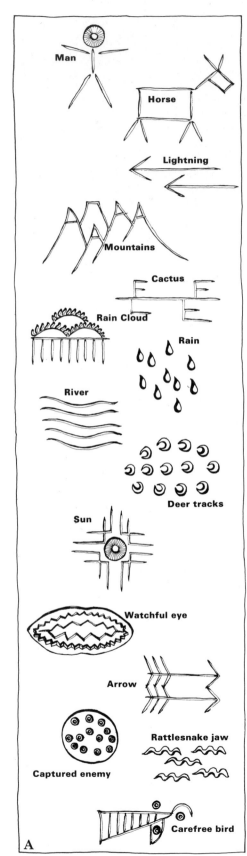

Figure A: Here are some of the authentic Navajo symbols you can arrange as you wish to make your belt tell a story.

Leathercrafts
Cowboy Belt

Of the many types of leather available, I think the best for making the cowboy belt pictured on page 40 are 200 to 250 gramme, vegetable-tanned leathers known as frenchback, bridleback, or spanishback. Latigo leather can be used, but it is sometimes too supple and it may stretch out of shape with wear—a characteristic of oil-tanned leathers. The vegetable-tanned hides are more rigid and longer lasting. They can take the wear and tear to which belts are subjected.

Leather is sold as whole hides or as splits (half hides). You need a split about 127 cm in length for a finished belt of 81-cm waist size. Longer waist sizes call for longer lengths. Place the hide smooth side up on any flat surface. With pencil and steel straightedge, mark off a line about 4.5 cm in from the long edge of the split. The length of the line depends on the size of belt you are making. For example, for an 81 cm waist, allow another 20 or 25 cm for overlap (depending on the number of fitting holes you will make—usually five). Allow another 5 or 7.5 cm for foldover at the buckle.

The width of your belt may be determined by the width of the buckle. Measure the belt width from the first line and draw another line parallel to the first line. Use the straightedge as a guide and cut along the two lines with the Stanley knife. Cut the ends of the belt square with the sides. Now trim all four edges with the No. 2 edger. It will remove just a sliver of the leather and leave a smooth bevelled edge. Photograph 3 shows the correct method of using the edger.

Now fold over about 5 or 7.5 cm of the leather at the end which will hold the buckle. Wet the fold area generously with a sponge first, then hammer the fold down with the buffalo-hide mallet. Now cut out the keeper—the little strip of leather folded over the belt and fastened to the back. It goes near the buckle, and functions as a first loop. The keeper is about 2 cm wide and 15 cm long.

2: Cut out belt, using Stanley knife. Make sure you have outlined belt correctly with your steel straightedge and pencil before you cut it out.

3: Using a No. 2 edger, trim all four sides of the belt. This edger is best for the purpose because it takes off just the right amount of leather.

After the keeper has been cut out, edge it as you did the belt. Then fit it around the belt and make a mark where the ends overlap. The area of overlap at each end must be skived—shaved at an angle—with the cobbler's knife so that when the ends are overlapped the area of overlap will be the thickness of a single piece of leather. Otherwise the overlap will be bulky, difficult to fasten to the belt, and uncomfortable when the belt is worn.

Prepare the belt for the buckle. For directions, see Craftnotes, page 48. The buckle goes on after you tool and stain the leather, but getting the belt ready for the buckle is done at this time. You are then ready for tooling. If you are not going to do any decorative tooling, you can proceed with the dyeing and finishing described later.

The tooling designs used on the cowboy belt were derived from original Navajo symbols shown in figure A. I made up a story as I went along. The symbols were mostly done freehand with tooling instruments, but a swivel knife can take the place of these tools. You can make up your own story with your own symbols, or arrange the symbols shown here any way you wish.

If you use the symbols shown, or others that have a definite top and bottom, you might consider the sex of the belt's wearer. Buckles on a woman's belt are traditionally at the left. On a man's belt the buckles are at the right. You will want the symbols to be right side up, and the story

4: With Stanley knife, cut out the keeper. Make it 2 cm wide, and no more than 15 cm long. Then trim all four sides with the No. 2 edger.

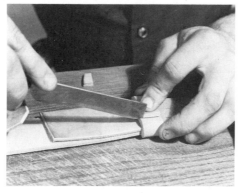

5: Mark the area of overlap on the keeper. Note that it is wrapped around the double thickness where the belt is folded for attaching the buckle.

6: Use your cobbler's knife to skive the overlap area at both ends of the keeper. When placed together, overlap area should equal the belt's thickness.

line (if used) to run in the right direction when the belt is worn. Work out your story beforehand to make sure that it will fit correctly.

My symbolized story is as follows: a man goes swiftly on a journey. He travels through some mountains to a desert, where he observes a good omen. This convinces him that he has bright prospects for the coming year. He has much to eat and drink and catches plenty of game, which makes him very happy. But he has need of caution, so he arms himself. When he meets his enemies, he conquers them. As a result he then feels tremendously strong, very confident and carefree.

To do the tooling, first dampen the entire belt with a wet sponge. Keep it moist at all times for pliability and ease of cutting. To make the cuts use the swivel knife as a chisel, and press the blade into the leather, first from one side of your pre-dawn design lines, and then from the other side. The two cuts will remove a small wedge of leather.

Dyeing and finishing

For dyeing and finishing, use the antique dyes and finishes, as these give a surface hardness that enhances the leather. Be sure to wear rubber gloves when dyeing because the dye is quite strong. Use a clean cloth to dot both sides of the belt with one coat of the light-brown paste dye. Place a coat of dark-brown antique paste dye over it. Now buff the belt with a piece of towelling or jersey, and let it dry before applying a coat of light or dark liquid dye (whichever you like better). I used the dark-brown liquid, and applied it by wetting a clean cloth with a little dye and daubing it on so as to produce dark spots here and there; this is a very good way to create the effect of age.

With your circular punch, make five holes for the buckle's tongue, about 2 cm apart. Join the skived ends of the keeper, and sew or rivet it in place (see Craftnotes, page 48, for riveting and sewing). Attach the buckle. Wet a cloth with finishing lacquer, and apply an even coat to the top surface. When it is dry, your belt is finished.

7: When dyeing the belt and keeper, be sure to wear rubber gloves. The best materials for buffing dyes and finishes are towelling or jersey rags.

Leathercrafts
Beaded Belt

By Ralph Perinchief

American Indians added bead and quill work to bandoliers and headbands. These designs were later used to decorate belts. This type of beadwork is usually couched on to leather—that is, the beaded design is made, then sewn on. The beaded design in this project is simpler than the traditional Indian designs used for belts but the beading will wear much longer than couched beading.

In addition to the tools and materials listed earlier for the cowboy belt project, you'll need a 1.8 m shoelace strip of leather and beads. Select beads with holes large enough for the leather lace to pass through, and the beads themselves must be larger than the holes you punch in the belt.

To start the design on the belt, first mark a point 12 or 15 cm from the keeper at the buckle end of the belt. This will allow for the overlap of the other end of the belt when it is buckled. Make a second mark about 5 cm in from the point where the last of the five holes will be punched. Measure between these two marks to determine how much space you have for the design. For example, if you have a 81 cm waist belt, you will wind up with about 61 cm for the design.

This design is composed of a series of elliptical stars made of leather lacing through the belt. There is a bead in the centre of each star and another bead midway between each pair of stars. Within the space you have reserved on the belt for the design, lay out in pencil the pattern of elliptical stars with holes midway between. The stars for this belt were spaced about 15 cm apart. The eight holes for the laces that will form each star are marked in the diamond shape shown in photograph 10. Note that there is a double hole in the centre of each star, and single holes along the belt's centreline midway between each star. After the pattern is completely laid out, you can punch the holes as in photograph 9.

Tie a knot in one end of the leather lace, then thread the other end up through the centre hole of the first star at one end of the belt. Bring the lace out to a perimeter hole, and thread it down, pulling it snugly against the face of your belt. Make sure the rough side of the lace lies flat against the smooth face of the belt. Thread the lace from the back of the belt up through the centre again, and out to the next perimeter hole, as pictured in photograph 11. Continue around the star's perimeter holes until all of its holes have been used.

8: Use a ruler and pencil to measure precisely the design for the beaded belt. Be sure to allow enough room at one end for closure holes and at the other for the buckle foldover.

9: After laying out the complete pattern of holes in pencil on the belt (see text), use the circular punch to make the actual holes. The pattern of holes will appear as in photograph 10.

Beads add interest, beauty and colour to a belt. You may use any number of colours and patterns. Here, the design has been worked with leather lacing and beads.

A buckle design you can copy by hammering eight brass rivets into a commercial leather-covered buckle. The technique of riveting is illustrated and described in Craftnotes, page 49.

Next, bring the lace up through the centre hole, as in photograph 12, thread a bead on to the lace, push the lace back through the centre hole, snug the bead against the belt. Then take the lace to the first hole between stars. Come up through the hole, add a bead, return to the back of the belt, and snug the bead. Repeat until the motifs have all been laced and beaded. Cut off excess lace after tying end of lace by working it under last section of lace, and knotting. Then cut off excess lace.

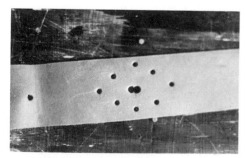

10: This is how the completed punch-out design should look. Note the single hole left of the star design, and the double hole in the centre of the star.

11: To begin weaving, bring leather lace up through centre hole, down through perimeter hole, up through centre again. Repeat until holes are filled.

When pulling lace through hole, keep it from twisting, and bring rough side of lace flush against smooth side of belt.

12: When all the holes in the belt are threaded, come up through centre again, thread last bead on to the lace, return to the back of the belt and then knot.

13: This is how the first beaded section of the belt should look when finished. Note how the leather lace moves from one motif to the next along underside of belt.

45

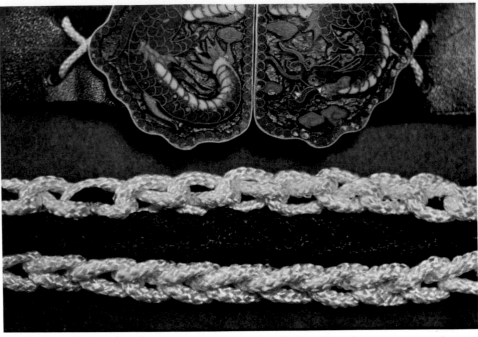

Using black and white nylon cord, or any combination of colours you choose, you can make a simple rope belt. Buckle partly visible above is made of chrome and stained glass.

A sampling of old buckles all using the Chimera or fabulous monster theme. Top one dates back almost 3,000 years; that at lower left is from A.D. 1000; the third is an 18th-century version.

Leathercrafts
Belts of Elastic

Many materials besides leather can be used for making a belt. These range from the precious (gold and silver) to the common (a strand of rope). Some of the most interesting belts you will encounter today are actually made from the simplest of materials.

One interesting material for a belt is elastic, which you can buy in plain white, or a variety of colours. A sewing centre, or any shop that sells dressmaking accessories, will have the type of elastic you need. You can buy one wide strip, or narrower strips in different colours. If you want a plain white or one-colour belt, it is all but complete when you buy the elastic. You just attach a buckle at one end, and insert grommets for the tongue holes at the other end. Or, as an alternative, you can stitch strips of leather to each end of a piece of elastic, then attach a buckle to one strip of leather, and punch holes in the other leather strip.

If you want a belt of different-coloured strands of elastic, buy the elastic in narrow widths, and stitch the edges together with elastic thread so the seams, as well as the material, will stretch.

14: With the single strand of black cord, make a slip knot. Through the loop, slip the oncoming cord to make a second loop, as in chain stitch crocheting.

15: Do not pull cord too tight as you make the series of loops. But be sure that each loop is pulled fairly snugly around the base of the succeeding loop.

16: A 12.5 cm unknotted section at end of each strand is used to secure the black strands to the white strands, and the white strands to the leather belt ends.

17: To secure the last loop at the end of each strand, pass the free end of the cord through the loop and pull it up snug. Then add a second hitch if desired.

18: Interweave free ends of black strands through parallel white strands on each side until you have taken care of all loose ends. Secure each with a knot.

You can add a beaded design, leather stitching, or other ornamental work, but not directly to the elastic. Do any such work on separate pieces of material—cloth or leather—and then couch (sew) these on to the elastic, as described in the entry under Beadwork.

The rope belt shown here is made of the nylon cord used for macramé. The cord can be bought at any needlecraft shop, and at most general handicraft shops. You can use any reasonable number of strands and colours. The belt illustrated is made of three strands, two white and one black. Each strand is a 5.5 m strip of nylon cord. When this cord is worked as described below, a 5.5 m strand will make a 61-cm length of belt.

Starting the belt

Make a slip knot 12.5 cm from an end of one white cord. Reach through the loop and pull through cord to form a second loop, in the manner of the basic crochet chain stitch. Continue pulling until the first loop is snug—but not too tight—around the base of the second loop. Reach through the second loop, and pull through a third, bringing the second up around the base of the third loop. Continue until only 12.5 cm are left at the other end of the cord. Pull this end through the last loop formed, to secure it. Repeat this process with the second white nylon cord.

Cut the black cord into three equal lengths, and repeat the process above with each piece. Leave 12.5 cm at both ends of each piece. Now you have two white and three shorter black chains. Lay the two white strands parallel to each other. Between them, end to end, lay the three strands of black cord. Several centimetres of white strands will be extending beyond the ends of the two outside black strands when these are butted against the ends of the middle black strand. Centre the black strands so the white extension is equal at both ends. Take the left free end of the left black strand, lace it down through a loop of an adjacent white strand, under and across to the other white strand, and up through a loop there. Bring this end back to the black strand, bring it down through first loop and tie it off by working strands through each other and then knotting.

Repeat with the right free end of the same strand, and with the free ends of the other two black strands. The black strands are now secured, by their ends, between the two white strands. To mount the buckle and provide holes for the buckle tongue, you need leather strips at either end of the elastic cord belt. To attach these strips, punch holes in one end of each leather strip and thread the free ends of the white cord through the holes. Tie knots in back, on the underside of the leather. The final size of the belt is determined by the length of the leather strips. Attach the buckle as you would on any leather belt. (See Craftnotes that follow.)

For information on related projects, see American Indian Crafts, in the *Acrylics . . .* volume.

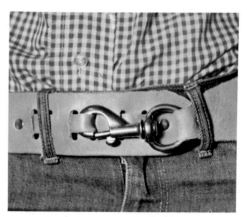

Your local hardware shop can provide this chain-snap, which you in turn can make into a buckle. Just follow the simple procedures for riveting a buckle which are described in Craftnotes (page 49).

BELT-BUCKLE CRAFTNOTES

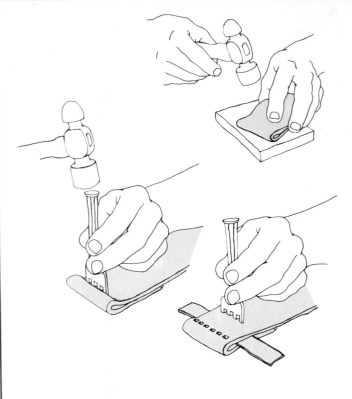

Leather shops sell a wide variety of buckles, many of them quite unusual. But you may enjoy searching for offbeat materials, as I often do, with which to improvise your own buckles. There are two basic methods for attaching a buckle to a belt. The first is by sewing. For this you need heavy-duty waxed thread, the four-pronged thonging chisel (or an awl), and a heavy needle.

When you cut out the cowboy belt (pages 42 and 43), you left some leather at one end for overlap, and at the other or buckle end for foldover. Work with the buckle end now.

Wet the leather thoroughly along the fold area, and make the foldover. Hammer with the buffalo-hide mallet or ball-peen hammer until the fold is smooth and flat, as shown in the top sketch on this page.

Use the four-pronged thonging chisel and your hammer to make four holes through both layers of leather, about 12 mm in from the fold. Then overlap the chisel on two of the holes and hit it again with the hammer. This gives you a total of six holes, as is shown in the sketch second from the top.

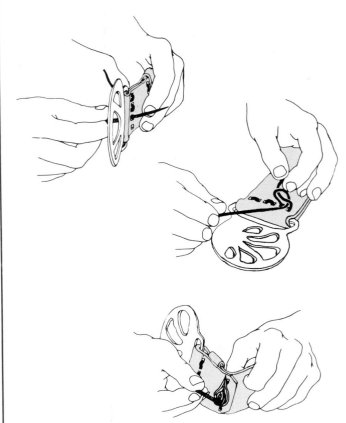

Now slip the keeper you made (see page 43) between the folds and position it fairly close to the row of six holes. Use the punch to make four holes on the other side of the keeper, for the final stitching that will hold it in place. (Since there is less strain here, you don't need six holes although you can use six for appearance.) By positioning the keeper between the folds, you can make sure the two rows of holes will not be too close together. Remove the keeper, bend it to form a loop, then rivet the ends together, following procedures described on the opposite page. Slip it off the belt, position the buckle, and return the keeper to its place between the two rows of holes.

After the holes for the tongue have been punched in the opposite end, and the tooling, dyeing, and buffing are done, it is time to sew keeper and buckle into place. With the waxed nylon thread, sew a single row of over, under, over stitches through the holes you made with the thonging chisel. Before you begin, be sure to make a tight knot at the end of the thread. When you have finished sewing, knot and cut the end of the thread as shown in last sketch on this page. Seal both ends by melting the wax with a match. While the wax is still malleable, press a little piece of metal, called an anvil, against it, to seal it, as you would seal a letter with sealing wax. Repeat the process with the second row of holes, and the buckle and keeper will then be secured to your belt.

Riveting is the other basic method used to attach a buckle to a belt. The easiest way to do it is with the small brass male-female rivets that are sold by leather crafters and at the d-i-y counters of department stores. You'll need a small piece of metal to serve as an anvil. Riveting is the method used to attach the buckle shown on page 47. The belt this buckle is attached to was made following the methods described on pages 42 and 43. The buckle was improvised. It is a simple brass chain snap of the type sold by regular and marine hardware stores.

Attaching the snap
To attach the chain snap, begin by measuring the width of the closed end of the lock side, then with a replaceable-blade knife, cut the end piece that will be folded under, as illustrated by the sketch at the top of this page.

With a circular punch, make three holes in the triangular end (for location of these holes, see the fourth sketch from top of page). Fold the triangular end under, hammer it as shown in third sketch from top of page, then press the circular punch through the three holes already made to create matching holes on the underside.

Riveting
To set the first rivet into its hole, place the anvil together with one half of the rivet under the belt, as illustrated in the fourth sketch. Press the holes in the belt down over the rivet. Press the second half of the rivet down on to the first half, then, using a rivet setter as shown, hammer the rivet closed.

Forming the loops
The snap buckle cannot be used with the type of holes customarily punched into belt ends. Instead, form a series of leather loops on which to catch the snap. Begin by cutting six rectangular slots about 2 cm apart into the belt end.

Next, cut out a strip of leather about 15 cm long, and about 12 mm wide. Slip it through the slots, starting from the back of the belt at one end, and lace it in, then out, then in, to form three loops at the belt front, as in the fifth sketch from the top of the page. Pull it tight enough so that just one loop, about 12 mm deep, can be formed, then rivet each end of the strip to the belt. If the strip is taut when you rivet it, you have defeated its purpose. You should instead be able to pull out a half-inch loop at any one of the three positions on the front of the belt. The sketch exaggerates slackness to make this point. Try the loop with your finger after fastening first end and before fastening second.

To fasten the belt, just pull out a loop and hook the snap lock to it. If the belt is to be made for a growing child, cut more slots and use a longer strip.

Buckles can be made of many materials other than metal. You can make a buckle of leather, heavy-duty plastic, wood, bone, almost anything strong enough to stand the pressure of a buckle pulled tight. Many of the materials lend themselves to decorative treatments by carving, painting, engraving, and other craft skills.

BICYCLES
The Toy That Grew Up

By John Savage

In the history of technology, the bicycle is probably a unique machine. Other inventions have come along, served mankind for a time, and then all but disappeared. Remember the windmill? The airship? The steam engine? These things don't count in our lives today. The bicycle, however, came along about 150 years ago, developed into a serious form of adult transport by the turn of this century, and then largely vanished as motor cars became a national mania.

For 50 years, the bicycle was considered little more than a toy for youngsters. Then, in the early 1960s, it made a comeback. Within a decade, Americans, for instance, were buying more bikes each year than cars (something that hadn't happened since the turn of the century). Nearly half of them were adult bikes, too. Today, about 18 million English people own bikes ranging from rusty relics to ultra-smart models.

There is a reason for this renaissance: the bicycle is a good idea. It is second only to the dolphin in efficiency of movement. You and your bike use less energy per pound per mile than does any other machine. The bicycle is a good idea for other reasons, too. It provides good exercise for a country with lots of leisure and little outlet for physical energy. For some, in cities or commuting, it provides a way to beat traffic jams. It does not pollute the air. It is inexpensive. And it gives people the satisfaction of depending on their own physical resources.

The strange idea that wouldn't die

How did anyone get the idea of balancing on a bar between two in-line wheels while rolling along? That idea must have been more bizarre in the 18th century than the unicycle is to us. The concept of self-propelled transportation hadn't really occurred to anyone until then. In the 1790s, the Comte de Sivrac, in Paris, invented a vehicle like a bicycle, except that it could not be steered. He sat astride the bar and pushed with his feet. When he started to fall, he caught himself with his feet. He obviously never thought about balancing indefinitely.

In Germany, a few decades later, Baron von Drais started building bike-like vehicles. For some reason lost to history, he made a front wheel that would steer. In 1817, he learned to do what nearly every child has learned—to ride and steer a two-wheeled bike.

It was still a push type (pedals were a long way off), but he could coast down long hills without ever touching his feet to the ground for balance. He had discovered that when you turn into a fall, you can recover your balance quite easily.

Von Drais called his bicycle a draisine, after himself. The machine caught

Ladies of the wheel have come a long way since this scene took place in 1896. Clothing styles have changed, but bicycles have remained much the same, with chain drive, pneumatic tyres and coaster brakes.

Cyclists enjoy the open road on lightweight ten-speed bikes. The boom in adult bicycling has made it a fast growing summer activity.

on among the nobility of Europe, especially in England. Everywhere, ladies and gentlemen were coasting around on these 34-kilo wooden monsters. They must have been fairly effective, because it was a long time before anyone got round to inventing pedals. Various inventors tried treadles and connecting rods, ratchets and gears, without lasting success. One man even invented a bike the rider lay down on while turning cranks with his hands. In 1863 the problem was overcome when the Michaux brothers, in Paris, simply put the pedals on the front wheel, like those you will find on a modern tricycle.

The big-wheel ordinaries

With the Michaux brothers' invention, cycling suddenly became very popular and spread throughout the world as a serious form of adult transportation. Bicycle racing also became a popular international sport. The competitive pressures of racing had a strange effect on bicycle design. The front wheel grew increasingly large, because pedalling one turn on a big wheel takes you farther than one turn on a small wheel. So big-wheel bikes beat little-wheel bikes. The wheels grew so big that only long-legged athletes could ride them. This bike, called the penny-farthing (from the comparison of the difference in size of the wheels to the coins of those names) or ordinary, was extremely unstable; a small rock could send the rider crashing head first.

The Lawson safety bike

The safety problem was solved in 1879 by Harry J. Lawson, in England. He invented the chain-and-sprocket drive, the kind we still use. Instead of making the wheel huge, he made the pedal sprocket large in comparison to the wheel sprocket. That way, he geared the bike so one turn of the pedals produced more than one turn of the wheels, accomplishing the same result as had the large wheel. This was known as the safety bicycle, and it soon replaced the high-wheeled ordinaries.

In 1888, Dr. John Dunlop, a Scotsman, invented the inflatable rubber tyre, which made bikes both faster and more comfortable. By the turn of the century, the bicycle had taken shape as we know it today, with coaster brake, multispeed hub gear, derailleur gear system, wire spokes, ball bearings, and steel frames. Bike design since 1900 has, for the most part, evolved around these refinements and the use of stronger, lighter metals.

Compared with the bicycles that existed 70 years ago, today's models weigh about half as much, perform more reliably, and actually cost less.

This ancestor of the bike was called a hobby-horse in 1823. The cyclist pushed on the ground with his feet and coasted.

The penny-farthing was the racing bike of the 1860s.

Fox hunting on bicycles instead of on horses was this cartoonist's way of satirising the world-wide bicycle mania at the turn of this century.

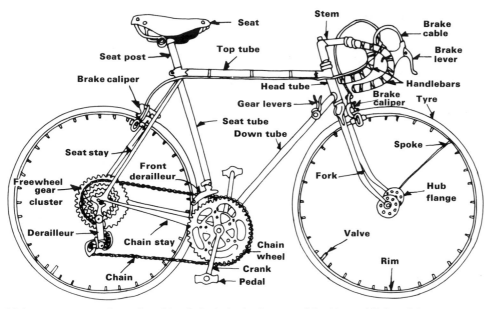

Major components of a modern bicycle include, in the case of the 10-speed lightweight, derailleurs and dropped handlebars.

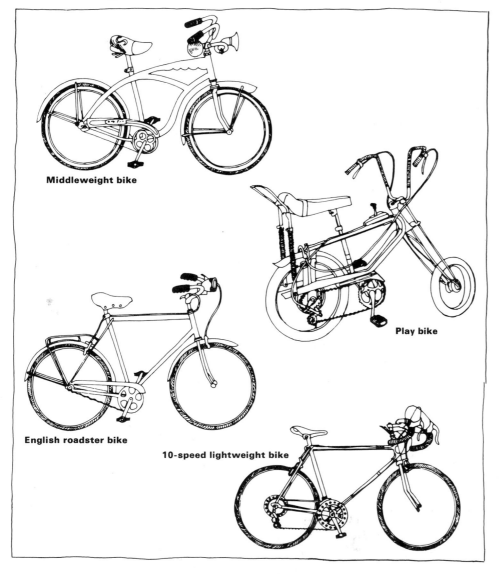

Middleweight bike

English roadster bike

Play bike

10-speed lightweight bike

How to choose the right bike

A benefit of the bike boom is the great variety of bicycle types available. You can choose from:

Middleweight bike: I don't know a heavier, harder-to-operate type than this 23 kilo bicycle that everyone over 40 grew up on. The largest, most common size has 66 cm wheels with balloon tyres (sizes 5.4 cm, 4.4 cm, and 3.5 cm), a reliable coaster brake, a welded steel frame, accounting for most of its cumbersome weight. The smallest middleweight has a 50 cm wheel with balloon tyres. You can get smaller sizes in solid-rubber tyres.

Play bike: There are many variations, but they all seem to have balloon tyres, 50 cm (more or less) wheels, a long banana seat, high-rise handlebars. Avoid models with handlebars higher than child's shoulder and a high U-shape bar extending behind the seat. Both can be hazardous. Play bikes are for rugged off-street play, and are not intended for highway use where they may cause accidents.

English roadster bike: This type, first developed in England, is now copied all over the world. Originally, it had a black lacquer finish, three-speed hub gear, hand brakes, a wicker basket on the handlebars. At 15 to 18 kilos, it weighs more than the 10-speed bike, but it is fine for exercise, commuting, and short jaunts.

10-speed lightweight bike: This type evolved in Europe during 50 years of international bicycle road racing, a sport which has become extremely popular. It also is the type that renewed adult interest in cycling.

Essentials are a very light frame of special alloy steel, dropped handlebars, narrow saddle, high-pressure tyres, and ten-gear combinations. These are changed by means of derailleurs, front and back; but derailleurs are more fragile than hub gears. These bikes weigh from 8 to 11 kilos.

The 10-speed bike sold in the United States costs less than most of those sold in Europe, but it is best for all-round use.

In 1886, tourists got a speeding ticket pedalling this tandem touring tricycle.

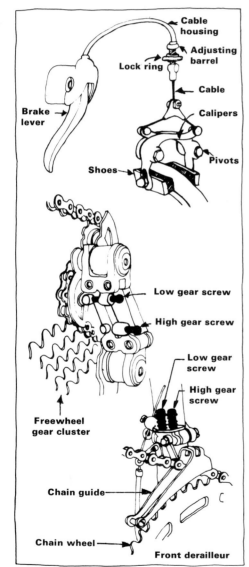

Above, parts of a typical hand brake assembly that are involved in owner adjustment and maintenance. Below adjustment screws on a typical rear (left) and front (right) derailleur. Text explains the adjustment procedures.

Cable housing

Adjusting barrel

Lock ring

Cable

Brake lever

Calipers

Pivots

Shoes

Low gear screw

High gear screw

Low gear screw

High gear screw

Freewheel gear cluster

Chain guide

Chain wheel

Front derailleur

Other bicycle types

Folding bikes, tandems (bicycles built for two), adult tricycles, cross-country bikes, delivery bikes, and unicycles are among the other types which are commonly in use today.

Folding bikes have a hinged frame to permit them to be stored in a cupboard or car boot. A normal or sports bicycle with a removable front wheel is, however, just as compact and is much easier to ride, as well as cheaper. Wing nuts on the front axle make wheel removal as easy as folding a folding bike.

Tandems are valuable when one member of a pair habitually outdistances and has to wait for the other. It permits both to cycle along together, while the stronger partner gets the desired amount of exercise.

Adult tricycles come in large sizes and with gears, but they are still somewhat hard to pedal. They are impossible to ride up a hill. However, if you cannot keep your balance on a two-wheeler and do not wish to cycle far, a tricycle is a solution.

What kind of bicycle for you?

Anyone over 1.60 metres tall should consider a 10-speed. For touring, commuting, exercising, or just riding around, it is the most suitable. A drawback is the delicacy of the derailleur system, which derails the chain from one sprocket to another to shift gears. However, all bicycle-gear systems require some care and adjustment. The 10-speed gives you a much more effective range of gears than three-speed hub gears, and it is worth taking the time to learn to shift, adjust, and care for it. The cost of a 10-speed bicycle ranges from under £44 to over £215. Beware of low-cost specials, which are usually heavy, ponderous, and mechanically troublesome; a 10-speed weighing over 12 kilos is probably a middleweight with derailleurs added. Avoid extra-high-pressure tubular racing tyres, the kind in which the tube and casing are integral. They are more fragile.

A second choice for adults is the English roadster type, preferably a standard make. The hub gear, which may have three to five speeds, is less fragile and requires less maintenance than the derailleur on a 10-speed bike. At a little under £44, the English roadster is a real bargain, considering the extent of its complicated machinery.

For a child, the choice depends on budget, the child's whims, and the availability of the bicycle desired. Most children are very hard on delicate parts, such as lights, speedometers, and gears. The main point in selecting youngsters' bikes is making sure they are the correct size for immediate use. If you get one that is too big (on the theory that the child will grow into it), he won't be able to control it as well as he should and will be more liable to accidents. Oversize bikes are a major cause of accidents among many children.

Making your bike fit

You don't have much choice as to size in the adult range. Wheel sizes of 66, 68.5, or, rarely, 71 cm are the only variables. Makers of expensive European bikes offer a choice of frame sizes, as well. The frame size is measured from the centre of the pedal axle to the top of the seat post. Sizes generally range from 53.5 to 66 cm. Your size is equal to the measure from inseam (crotch) to the floor, minus 23 or 25.5 cm. If you are 1.78 metres in height, you probably need a 56 cm-frame bicycle. Most American frames are 53 cm, because manufacturers there still tend to make bicycles with children in mind.

The most important adjustment is saddle height. Most cyclists set the saddle too low, which makes pedalling more tiring. The height is correct when the ball of your foot rests on the down pedal and your leg is almost straight but the knee is not locked. The nose of the saddle should be about 5 cm back of a vertical line extending up through the pedal axle—more if you have long legs. The stem of dropped handlebars should be adjusted to be slightly lower than the top of the saddle.

Maintenance and repair

The major problems of bicycle maintenance are dirt, water, and lack of oil or grease. Wipe your bike clean every week (more often if it gets very dirty) with a rag barely damp with paraffin; lubricate it regularly, and readjust things as they need it.

There are four things you should check before each ride: brakes, tyres, bolts, and gears. For coaster brakes (usually found on improved models and some small-wheel types), this means seeing that the brake arm is clamped to the chain stay and that the chain is not loose or broken. While you are at it, make sure the chain is clean; a dirty one can use 25 per cent of your pedal power. For cleaning, use an old toothbrush and a solvent such as paraffin then wipe completely dry, and soak with oil. Wipe chain nearly dry again to keep dust and dirt from clinging to excess oil.

For hand brakes and their levers, check the calipers for adjustment and

1: Front wheel must be aligned between forks and held tightly by nuts or release lever. Bearings (arrows) should be kept clean and lubricated with grease.

2: Rattrap pedals have sawtooth edges for better grip, but hurt feet in thin-soled plimsolls. Keep bearings oiled (arrow). Note reflectors on pedals.

3: Gear lever and cable are used a lot on tour. Keep a dab of grease on the cable (arrow) where it makes metal-to-metal contact or flexes.

4: Gear lever exerts great pull on cable when moving chain. Grease cable (upper arrow), and keep moving parts of derailleur oiled (lower arrow) and clean.

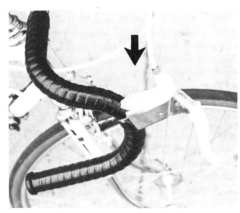

5: Brake levers must be kept adjusted and lubricated with grease. Crimp lever to expose cable inside for greasing (arrow). If cable starts to fray, replace.

6: Brake calipers must move freely and return quickly to open position. Wipe them clean after each ride, and put a drop of oil where the arrow indicates.

the brake shoes for wear. Replace worn or missing shoes. Adjust the calipers so the shoes are 5 mm or less from the rims. To do this, pinch calipers together, loosen lock ring at the end of the brake-cable housing, and turn the adjusting barrel to take up the slack. Then tighten lock ring again. Oil the brake and gear cables where they enter and leave the cable housings. Also, oil gear levers and the pivots of caliper brakes.

Inspect tyres regularly for wear and cracks, and check their pressure before each ride. Soft tyres can be cut or damaged by the rims, and they

8: Chain tension is correct when chain sags about a centimetre across top of sprockets.
Use spanner to loosen rear wheel and move it up or back to adjust chain tension.

7: Spoke spanner is used to adjust tension
of spokes and thereby align the wheel.
Truing a wheel is not difficult, but it takes
patience and careful attention.

are much harder to pedal. If the tyre's air valve is at an acute angle to the
rim, it may leak at its base after hard riding. Deflate the tyre; pull it
against the rim until the valve is straight; then reinflate the inner tube to
the proper pressure.

Before each ride, also make sure all bolts are tight and each wheel is
aligned between the forks. If it is not, loosen axle nuts; align wheel,
and tighten nuts again. If the wheel continues to rub against the fork despite
adjustments, take it to a cycle shop.

Gears need adjustment as cables stretch and parts wear. You adjust hub
gears at the right side of the rear axle, where the cable joins a chain or
lever that goes into the axle itself. Place gear lever (on handlebars) in
middle, also known as normal or 2, position. Loosen lock nut at wheel end of
shift cable, and turn adjusting barrel until the end of the chain (not the
cable) is even with the end of the axle.

The most common ailments of derailleur-gear systems on 10-speed bikes
occur when the chain (1) won't shift on to a large and/or small sprocket or
(2) does shift but goes off the other side. There are adjusting screws on
almost all front and rear derailleurs; check your instruction manual for
their locations.

To adjust the front derailleur, shift the chain on to the large sprocket
by turning the pedals. Adjust the high-gear screw until the chain guide
clears the chain on the outside by about 1 mm. Turn the pedals; shift
the chain on to the small sprocket, and adjust the low-gear screw for the
same clearance on the opposite side.

To adjust the rear derailleur, crank pedals, and shift chain to centre
sprocket of the rear wheel cluster. If the derailleur jockey wheel does not
line up with the centre of the chain, the derailleur mounting may be bent.
Straighten it with a spanner. Then turn pedals; shift chain on to the small
(high) gear sprocket, and keep turning to make sure it stays there. If it
won't go on the smallest sprocket, or goes on and off the other side, turn
high-gear adjusting screw until chain rides on the gear easily. Then shift
the chain to the largest sprocket, and make similar adjustments with the
low-gear adjusting screw.

Tyres and punctures

The hardest part of fixing a puncture is removing the wheel. First, turn the bike upside down, remove the axle nuts. Remember the order in which any washers, mudguard stays, and carriers come off. On rear wheels, slip the chain off the sprocket. In the case of hub gears, remove gear cable by loosening lock ring and turning adjusting barrel anti-clockwise until it is free. Coaster-brake arms are attached to the wheel stays by brackets. Remove arms and brackets from the wheel stays. Caliper brakes may have to be loosened to get the wheel out. Then slip the wheel out.

To get the tyre off, slip blunt screwdrivers or tyre levers between the tyre and the rim until the bead (inside edge) of the tyre is freed (photograph 10). Push the valve stem inside the rim. Then reach inside and pull the tube out of the tyre, working around the circumference carefully to keep from marring the tube.

Inflate the tube until it is about double its normal size. If you can't locate the leak by feeling the rushing air on your cheek, or hearing it, rotate the tube under water, and watch for bubbles (photograph 11). When you find the leak, clean and dry the area around it well. Then scratch the area with a roughing tool (photograph 12) so the patch you apply will grip better. Apply a thin coat of rubber cement over the roughened area; let dry thoroughly (photograph 13). Take a special rubber patch from puncture repair kit; remove the cloth backing that keeps its sticky side fresh. Place patch over cemented area. Then work the tube back into tyre (photograph 14) and free bead of tyre back well inside the rim.

9: Puncture repair kit and tyre levers are essential for touring. Kit has cement, roughing tool, and rubber patches. Tyre levers have rounded ends to save tubes.

10: Tyre levers in use. Pry one between tyre bead and rim carefully, so as not to tear the inner tube. Insert other lever and work both ways from centre.

11: Bubbles reveal holes in an inner tube when it is placed under water. Be sure the tube is completely dry before patch is applied, or the cement won't hold.

12: Roughing tool is used over hole to give the cement a better surface to stick on. If patch falls over the mould line on tube, line should be rubbed flush.

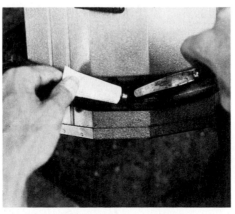

13: Apply rubber cement to roughed-up area around the hole. It should be applied very thinly and allowed to dry completely. Then rubber patch goes on.

14: Replace inner tube by inserting the valve first and working tube inside tyre both ways from centre. Then work free tyre bead back inside rim all around.

Bicycle touring

Bicycle touring is apparently here to stay. It isn't necessary to travel far to get real enjoyment out of cycle touring. Short trips in the U.K. or on the Continent, in small, family-size groups are fun.

Touring is more enjoyable if it is well planned. Even on a short trip, your route should be carefully worked out in advance. Avoid peak traffic periods, roads with heavy traffic, roads that don't permit bicycles. Some cities— Amsterdam for instance—have bike routes marked with signs, to make cycling safe. On some British main roads there are segregated cycle tracks, although there should be more. Where they exist—use them!

If possible, plan the trip to avoid very long or very steep hills. A longer level route may take less time than a short and hilly one. A 10-speed bicycle can go almost anywhere, however, so don't miss a scenic route just because there are a few hills along the way.

You can usually stay at youth hostels, pubs or at the home of a friend, but many people like to camp out. For protection against cold or rain, take a compact, lightweight sleeping bag and a waterproof ground sheet. A tent or cover is advisable. But keep the volume of gear to a minimum. Cycling against a wind, you can be worn out faster by the burden of a sleeping bag than by 5 kilos of extra gear.

For summer cycle camping, I suggest the following clothing: a pair of shorts; a pair of trousers; a long-sleeved shirt; a short-sleeved shirt; two pairs socks; two sets underwear; a sweater; a light anorak; a hat; gloves; cycling shoes; waterproof cycling cape. You don't need special cycling shoes, just shoes that are appropriate for pedalling. Thin-soled shoes against

rat trap pedals can be painful. Gloves can be light cotton work type or soft leather. They are needed for a long day of gripping handlebars.

For meals on a cycle tour, you can stop at road-side cafés or pubs. If you want to cook out, don't carry food from home; buy it along the way. Use the kind of cookware mountaineers use—small, light, and nesting. One plate, one cup, a knife, fork, and spoon should suffice each person.

For bike touring (even if it is not overnight), carry a few tools and parts. Tools include adjustable spanner, small and medium screwdrivers, tyre levers, small pliers, and any special spanners or tools that come with the bike. Take a puncture repair kit, a spare inner tube, and, for long trips, extra brake pads and cables for brakes and gears. When making repairs, get your bike completely off the road.

The way to carry your gear? The idea is to keep it low, with little bulk, and evenly distributed between the two wheels. Most convenient is a light metal carrier over the rear wheel. To this, strap on pannier bags of tough, water-resistant cloth. To distribute the weight better, use a small bag strapped to the handlebars. Don't wear a back pack; it makes bike handling dangerous. Keep the centre of gravity low.

Touring safety

Since bicycles usually have to share roads and highways with cars, a heightened sense of safety is wise. In a bicycle-car accident, the cyclist has more to lose no matter whose fault it is. Here are some pointers:
□ Ride on the same side of the road as the cars, going with the traffic.
□ Know the Highway Code, and obey it.

Rules for the road for bicycles are the same as for cars, with a few defensive rules added. Ride single file with car traffic. Learn the Highway Code for the country in which you are cycling.

- Ride single file and in a straight line.
- Be aware of traffic ahead of and behind you.
- Always signal your intentions well in advance, using hand signals.
- Wear light-coloured clothing at night.
- Equip your bike with 5 cm disc and pedal reflectors.
- When riding in town, watch out for parked car doors opening.
- On major roads, check the shoulders before you have to pull over for passing cars. Be wary if they are soft, gravelly, or full of ruts.
- Don't piggyback on a bike.
- Don't hold on to passing buses, trucks or cars.
- Give pedestrians and cars the right of way.
- In rain watch for greasy patches.

Bicycle clubs

In and around the country many local bicycle clubs are appearing and if you are thinking of joining one or starting one of your own, several specialized organisations can provide information.

The Cyclists' Touring Club is the oldest and largest organization of its kind in the British Isles, with over 23,000 members in 1974. There are 50 district associations which are divided into local area groups. The Club offers its members a bi-monthly newsletter along with information on forthcoming cycling events and activities, which include touring holidays: these are usually parties of 12-16 people, who may tour the British Isles or the Continent. It also produces an annual handbook in early March, which has a section containing approximately 3,000 addresses of hotels and guest houses throughout the British Isles, information on cycle repairers, and items of interest to the keen cyclist. (This is available to non-members for a nominal fee.) Membership is £2.60 for adults, junior membership (18-20) £1.87, and children's membership £1.25. There is also a family membership which costs 54 pence for each member of the family under 18 so long as one parent has paid an adult subscription. The Club's national headquarters are at Cotterell House, 69 Meadrow, Godalming, Surrey GU7 3HS.

Youth Hostels of England and Wales, a national organization with affiliates all over the country, is not specifically a bicycling organization, but a large number of its members use bicycles for excursions. The YHA maintains inexpensive accommodation for travellers—in old schools, National Trust mansions, castles, farmhouses or specially built premises. Members pay as little as 50 pence for overnight lodging, and cooking facilities are usually available. Based on a concept that originated in Germany in 1909, the YHA now has 10 regional councils around England and Wales, and will also put you in touch with hostel associations in 48 countries throughout the world.

The organization provides members with passes for any of its world-wide facilities; along with a handbook (available to non-members for 20 pence) they can advise you of the adventure holidays they organize, which include cycling holidays; lectures and films. At the YHA people of all ages are welcome. A family membership which includes children under 15 is £3.30; junior membership is 55 pence (5-15 years old), and £1.10 (16-20 years old.) Adult membership is £1.65. For more information, write to the Youth Hostel Association of England and Wales, Trevelyan House, St. Albans, Hertfordshire.

Other national organizations serve more specialized interests. The British Cycling Federation caters for the racing enthusiast as well as the general cyclist, and affiliated clubs organize road racing and track racing competitions throughout the country. There are also clubs for people whose main interest is both collecting and riding antique bicycles. The largest of these is the Southern Veteran Cycle Club which arranges occasional meetings and races, and also publishes a quarterly magazine called The Boneshaker. Details can be obtained from Mike Roberts, 87 Hitchings Way, Reigate, Surrey.

Map reading is an important part of cycle touring. Remember that the energy wasted by getting lost is your own. Plan cross-country trips carefully in advance.

Once you receive a list of district cycling organizations from the Cyclists'
Touring Club, you might find that there is no club in your neighbourhood.
Why not set about organizing your own? By becoming affiliated to the
Cyclists' Touring Club you will gain advice on how to organize your first
meeting, how to publicise your new club, and how to establish its objectives
(should it cater for tourers or racers; should it be involved in trying to
obtain local legislation for safer cycling facilities?) Two other
organizations which may be of help in these matters are the British Cycling
Bureau, Greater London House, Hampstead Road, London N.W.1, and the
Bicycle Association of Great Britain, Stanley House, Eaton Road,
Coventry, Warwickshire.

One way to create interest in a new club, or just to have fun, is to
organize a bicycle holiday. Select a three-day weekend in spring or early
summer. Be sure to plan far in advance: two months of planning are not
really too much when you think of all the things you will have to do. Work
out the route well beforehand, avoiding busy road intersections if possible—
if not, always ask the police or traffic wardens to assist at a crossing. This is
a family event, so when you plan the route, make sure it is not too difficult
for "rusty" cyclists! Allow time for lunch, and finish each day in time for
dinner. Draw up a simple map showing points of interest and distances. Help
in doing this can be obtained from one of the local information officers
mentioned in the C.T.C. handbook. Hand it out to each cyclist, together
with a leaflet indicating the date, time, and starting place.

Joining a bicycle club is a great way for the family to meet people who are interested
in touring, racing, and the special problems of better cycle tracks.

BIRDS AND BIRDHOUSES
Friends from the Wild

By Jeremiah J. Thibault

For pet fanciers, the fanciest pets you can have, and the easiest to care for, are wild birds. They are free for the friendship you offer, and they don't arouse the sense of guilt you would suffer in keeping most wild pets. Even if casually neglected, the wild bird can fend for himself. But if permanently neglected, he will depart for more desirable surroundings.

The easiest kind of bird-watching is through windows in your kitchen or near your dining-room table. The yard or garden beyond will be a refuge for birds if certain conditions are met. Protect the birds from cats by screening off, perhaps with a tangle of thorny hedge plants, open spaces where cats usually wander. Wrap tree trunks with painted aluminium bands to prevent cats from climbing. The metal is painted a colour similar to that of the tree's bark, and will not spoil the garden's natural look. Shields also cut down squirrel raids on nests and feeding stations.

Providing food and water

Water for drinking and bathing is essential to birds, so provide a birdbath. Set it in a protected spot. An open area is best, preferably one surrounded by thorny bushes to keep away predatory animals.

The diet of most wild birds consists of berries and insects—birds definitely help to control the insect problem. Birds should be well fed in wintertime, when snow covers their usual sources of supply, but should be fed only sparingly in the summer. If you set out a lot of grain when natural foods are available, the birds will become too dependent on you. In good weather, offer enough food to attract birds to your area, but leave them hungry enough to hunt for more on their own. At one time the experts suggested regular feeding, even in summer, but now advise restraint. The recent interest commercial enterprises have shown in packaging wild-bird food has created too thriving a market. Bell-shaped clusters of millet and sunflower seeds, sacks of loose grain, even instant feeders of waxed cardboard are available in many supermarkets and pet shops. It is all too easy for bird lovers to buy these and simply overdo a good thing. Buy some, yes, but don't go overboard. Too much will not only lessen the survival capability of the birds you find desirable, but will attract hordes of sparrows, pigeons, and untidy starlings. Squirrels, too, will get into the act, as will the beautiful but pugnacious jay and magpie. Many people like jays and go to lengths to attract them, but they can be a real nuisance; they strip your garden of young peas, beans and similar vegetables, leaving you nothing to show for your labour.

Plant trees and shrubs

A good lawn, surrounded by shrubs and a few trees, will encourage numerous birds to your garden. Cotoneaster and berberis are much enjoyed by thrushes and blackbirds. The lime, honeysuckle and holly are very popular with insect-eating birds; members of the tit family, warblers and some finches supplement their normal diet of seeds in this way.

A family of jays inspects the freshly cast birdbath, set on a tree stump in this quiet garden. Note the birdhouse top, bird feeder (beyond table), and ample foliage.

Environmental Projects
Blue Tit House

A

Figure A: Bluetits are easily driven from home by more aggressive birds. The 3.5 cm hole excludes starlings; the inside perch discourages sparrows.

An excellent way to attract wild birds to your property is to provide them with a place where they would like to live. Different kinds of birds prefer different types of homes and different locations. The plans presented here will accommodate the blue tit, the wren, and the purple martin; each requires a slightly different environment. Blue tits prefer quiet, open locations, about 2 m above the ground and facing south. Males claim territories and will fight any blue tits nesting within a couple of hundred yards. That sets a limit of only one blue tit house for yard or garden.

This is the simplest of the birdhouse projects, requiring only hammer, saw, and drill. These plans show it made of pine board which is 2 cm thick, but you can easily adapt them for plywood of almost any thickness. Cut all parts accurately. The inside perch discourages intruders and is a convenience for the baby blue tit. Start by nailing two sides to the bottom, and nail that to the back. Then nail on the front, making sure the outer top edge is a little higher than the top line of the sides. This, with the spacer slat, nailed to the sides, provides small air vents. Put the roof in place, and nail the holding slat tightly against it, but not to it. Insert a screw eye through the roof into the front. Once a year, you can loosen and remove the roof for cleaning the house. Finish house with stain or paint, or protect it with wood preservative and leave it to weather naturally.

Figure B: Measure and cut pieces from a piece of 2 by 20.5 cm board, 1.5 m long.

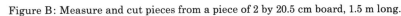

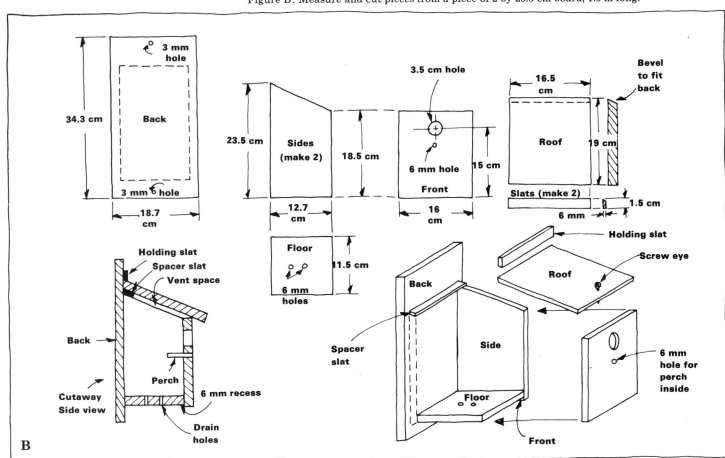

B

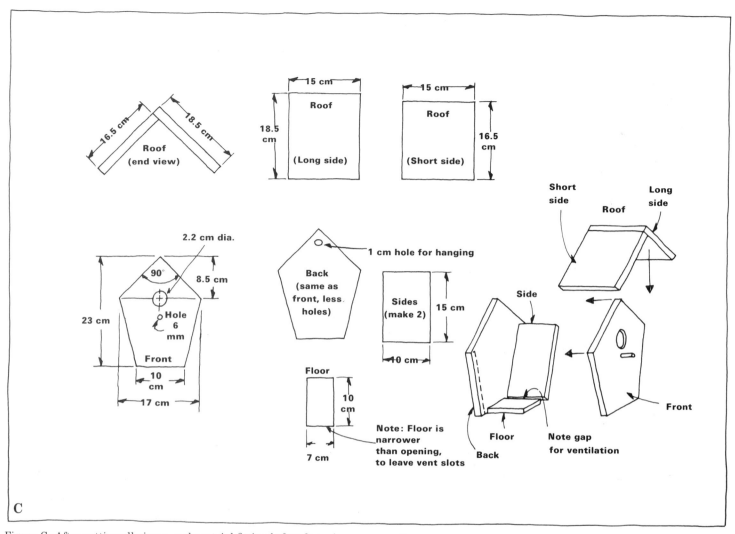

Figure C: After cutting all pieces, make a trial fitting before fastening permanently.

Environmental Projects
Wren House

The perky little wren seems to have adapted to suburban life as well as people have. It may, of course, prefer a hole in an ancient apple tree, but it seems to appreciate a well-made house like this one. Size of the entrance hole is important, because a larger one would let in larger birds. A wren house should be placed 2 to 3 m above the ground, on a tree trunk or the side of a house. Wrens do not mind higher locations, however.

Construction is straightforward, all pieces being cut from one 1.2-m length of 2 by 20.5 cm board.

Use galvanised 4 cm nails throughout. If desired, apply wood preservative to the parts before you assemble the house.

Install the perch in the front before assembling. It is made from a 6 mm dowel, 5 cm long. A touch of glue will make it more secure.

To assemble: Nail sides to back. Then fit and nail the floor, noting that there is a space on each side for drainage and ventilation. Then nail on the front. The roof is made by butting the short side against the long one and nailing them together. Then nail the roof to the front and back pieces. If you wish, the floor can be attached with No. 6 wood screws, 4 cm long, so it can be easily removed for cleaning the house.

Figure D: Wren house is decorative as well as practical for your garden. These cocky birds eat quantities of beetles, bugs, caterpillars and other insects.

Building a Bird Feeder

This jumbo bird feeder is larger than ordinary commercial feeders, which means you can feed more birds and go longer between refills. The glass sides form a hopper, which constantly replenishes the food in the tray by gravitational action. Glass is used so that you can tell when the feeder needs refilling without having to open it and look inside.

The first step in construction is to cut the tray and the tray side and end rails. Then assemble them as shown in figure F on the opposite page. Note that the tray corners are nipped off to provide drainage. The tray rails are made of 1.3-cm-thick stock.

Cut the two end pieces as shown, and make the grooves for the glass. These are just double saw cuts 4 mm deep. Rake out these grooves, and make sure the glass will slip into them before you assemble the feeder. Then attach the end pieces to the tray, directly to the end rails. Use galvanized 4 cm nails or brass screws.

The next step is to cut the glass, which is best done by your hardware or glass merchant shop. Slip it in place in the grooves in the end pieces, letting it rest on the top edge of the end rails so there is space for the food to spill out. If it rides higher than the top of the end piece, simply cut away a little of the end rails with a penknife to lower it. With glass roof in place, fasten the centre piece of the roof, as shown. Then fasten one roof side piece. Each roof side piece must have the edge bevelled where it meets the centre piece.

Fit the hinged roof section, and fasten hinges with screws. If you want the feeder to be waterproof, cut a piece of asphalt roofing paper (tar paper) to cover roof area, including hinged section. Fasten it with galvanized tacks to both sides of roof. Insert large screw eyes through each end of the fixed roof and into end pieces, for hanging the feeder. For mounting on a pole, omit screw eyes; attach with angle irons to bottom of tray.

Each suet holder is cut from two pieces of wood 2 cm thick, glued together with waterproof glue. After you cut them, mark holes for the three holding pegs (7.5 cm lengths of 6 mm dowel); drill holes, and insert the pegs. The holders can easily be removed for refilling, since they are held in place on the pegs with rubber bands or string. Whether you hang the feeder or mount it on a pole, be sure you can get at it for easy refilling. And have it near a window, especially where you can watch it while you are eating breakfast. There is nothing like breakfasting with the birds.

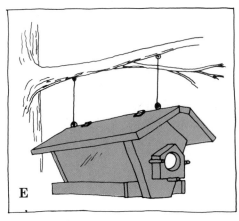

Figure E: Hang the bird feeder from a tree limb or from a piece of 5 by 10 cm wood, nailed to the corner of the house, or mount it on a pole.

Tapping a suet block into place on the jumbo bird feeder. The unit is shown mounted on a pole above auxiliary feeding trays.

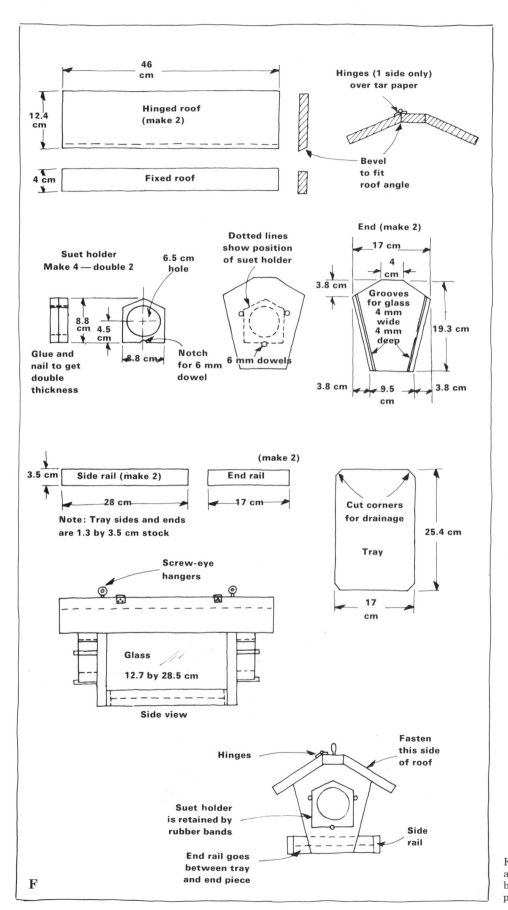

46 cm

Hinged roof (make 2)

12.4 cm

4 cm

Fixed roof

Hinges (1 side only) over tar paper

Bevel to fit roof angle

Suet holder Make 4 — double 2

6.5 cm hole

8.8 cm

4.5 cm

8.8 cm

Glue and nail to get double thickness

Notch for 6 mm dowel

Dotted lines show position of suet holder

6 mm dowels

End (make 2)

17 cm

4 cm

3.8 cm

Grooves for glass 4 mm wide 4 mm deep

19.3 cm

3.8 cm

9.5 cm

3.8 cm

3.5 cm

Side rail (make 2)

End rail

(make 2)

28 cm

17 cm

Note: Tray sides and ends are 1.3 by 3.5 cm stock

Cut corners for drainage

Tray

25.4 cm

17 cm

Screw-eye hangers

Glass

12.7 by 28.5 cm

Side view

Hinges

Suet holder is retained by rubber bands

End rail goes between tray and end piece

Fasten this side of roof

Side rail

Figure F: The parts needed for the feeder are shown here. Cut all of them carefully before you start assembly. Use a wood preservative to ensure longer life.

F

67

Environmental Projects
Dove and Pigeon Cotes

Mount the dove cote as high as possible—
3 to 5 metres—on a pipe or wooden post.
Just be sure you can get to it safely for
seasonal cleaning.

Doves and pigeons are especially fond of communal living, and this multiple dwelling is ideal for them. Although it is an ambitious project, it is still within the scope of modest skills. The finished house should be placed about 3 to 5 m high. A length of threaded 3.2 cm iron pipe, set in concrete and with a flange for mounting the house, is ideal.

Cut all pieces carefully, and apply a finish before assembly. Wood preservative is sufficient, although many people like to paint birdhouses to look like their own homes. First, attach the first floor to the base, with grains running at right angles to prevent warping. Inside partitions are like egg crates and are made from 1.3 cm pine or plywood, cut as shown in figure H. No fastenings are necessary; the slots hold pieces together. Attach ledges before assembling.

Fasten one side and one end on to the first floor permanently, using 4 cm galvanized nails. Fasten the corner. Put the first-floor partitions in place, and lay the second floor over them. Put in the second-floor partitions, and lay the third floor on top. All these pieces above the first floor go in place without permanent fastening. Next, fasten the other end and side permanently. Fasten corner boards permanently. Use 4 cm brass screws to hold the roof on—so it can be removed for cleaning. The interior floors and partitions will lift out and can be put back easily.

Figure G: Exploded view of the dove cote shows the outer nesting sections, the central shaft for ventilation, and how the house is assembled.

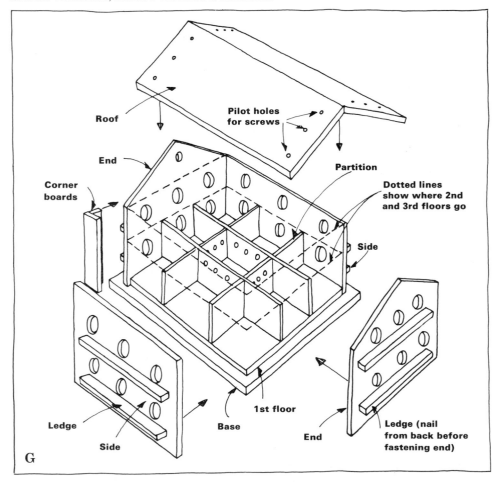

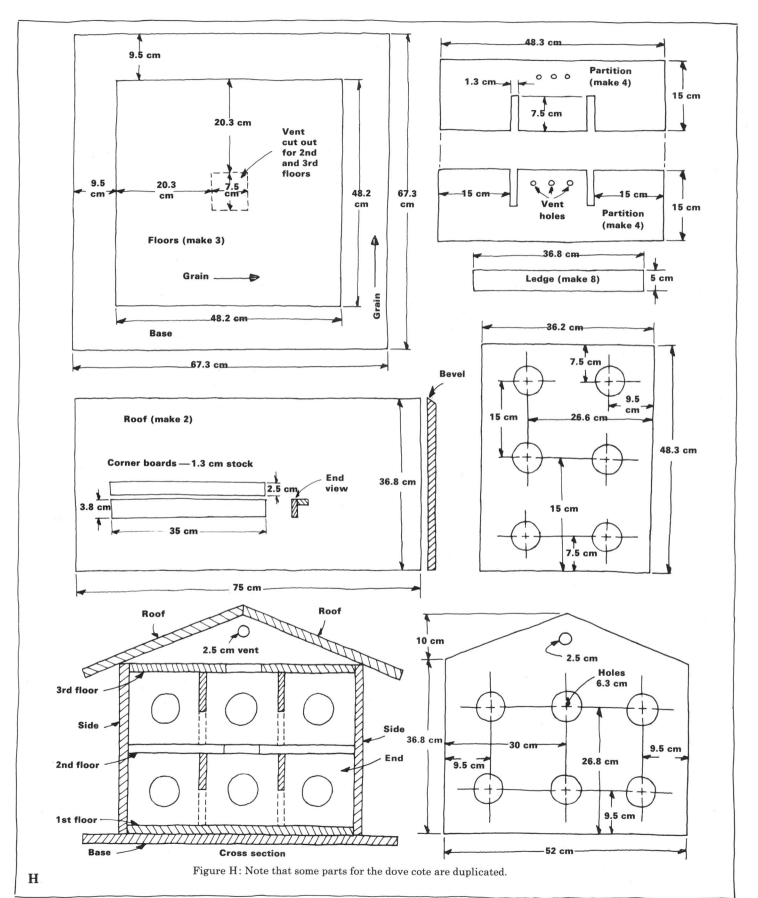

9.5 cm

20.3 cm

Vent cut out for 2nd and 3rd floors

9.5 cm

20.3 cm

7.5 cm

48.2 cm

67.3 cm

Floors (make 3)

Grain

Grain

48.2 cm

Base

67.3 cm

48.3 cm

1.3 cm

Partition (make 4)

15 cm

7.5 cm

15 cm

15 cm

Vent holes

Partition (make 4)

15 cm

36.8 cm

Ledge (make 8)

5 cm

36.2 cm

7.5 cm

9.5 cm

15 cm

26.6 cm

48.3 cm

15 cm

7.5 cm

Bevel

Roof (make 2)

Corner boards — 1.3 cm stock

2.5 cm

End view

3.8 cm

36.8 cm

35 cm

75 cm

Roof

Roof

2.5 cm vent

10 cm

2.5 cm

3rd floor

Holes 6.3 cm

Side

Side

2nd floor

End

36.8 cm

30 cm

9.5 cm

1st floor

9.5 cm

26.8 cm

9.5 cm

Base

Cross section

52 cm

Figure H: Note that some parts for the dove cote are duplicated.

H

69

Making a Concrete Birdbath

The simplest way to make a practical birdbath is to use the cover from a plastic dustbin as a form, fill it with mixed concrete, and either scoop out a shallow space for the bowl, as the concrete begins to harden, or form one with the bottom of a dustbin.

The birdbath pictured on the opposite page was moulded in a medium-size plastic lid. It measured 50 cm across the top, a suitable size. Lid depth, measured from a stick laid across the rim, was 7.5 cm. As the photographs show, the cover, upside down, was set on the dustbin. Since the weight of the concrete might collapse the can, it was filled two-thirds full of water to support and stiffen it.

A look at the form showed that a slight indentation in the centre of the lid would make a bump on the bottom of the casting, and that would make the finished birdbath unsteady. An octagon large enough to cover the indentation was cut from a stiff piece of rubberized-asbestos roofing material and fastened in place with masking tape. Locking tabs at lid sides and handle openings also had to be covered. A strip of scrap aluminium was taped over each opening (photograph 2). This made the circle slightly imperfect, but not enough to be concerned about. Then the form was lined with a piece of plastic sheeting, on to which the mixed concrete was shovelled (photograph 3). This was to make it easier to remove the hardened casting from the lid. The plastic was peeled off when concrete had set.

1: You need asbestos patch, dustbins, a cover, a bag of sand mix, basin, trowel, wire mesh, masking tape, wire cutters.

2: Almost fill plastic dustbin with water to stiffen it. Cut aluminium strips to cover holes, and tape them down.

3: To make it easier to remove the hardened casting from the lid, lay plastic sheeting over the cover mould.

4: Pour one-third of sand-mix concrete into pan, and stir well while dry. Add half a litre of water, and mix thoroughly.

5: Shovel mixed concrete into mould resting on water-filled can. Spread to form a bottom layer of 2 cm thickness.

We used about two-thirds of a 4.5 kilo bag of sand mix, mixed in two batches. One-third of the sand mix was poured into a large basin and stirred, dry, with a spade (photograph 4). You could mix it in a metal wheelbarrow.

About half a litre of water was added and mixed in thoroughly. The fairly stiff mix was shovelled into the form and spread evenly. To forestall cracking, a piece of chicken wire was cut with tin snips into a rough circle and laid on the first 2 cm layer of concrete (photograph 6). The rest of the batch was added, covering the wire. At this point, the form was half-filled.

6: Reinforce bottom with piece of coarse wire mesh or chicken wire. Snip to size, and press down into wet concrete in mould.

7: Add another 1.5 cm of wet concrete over wire reinforcement. Set the second can firmly into form, centring it.

8: Put about 10 cm of water in top can, to hold it in place. Now shovel in second mix of concrete to fill sides.

9: Smooth sides with trowel. Round edge with edger if you have one. Oil mould or line it with plastic for easier removal.

Finished birdbath has fluted interior design, rounded edging, and an appealing pool of water. Birds will take to it.

Another dustbin, right side up, was then set into the form (photograph 7) and was anchored in place by putting about 4.5 litres of water into it. If only one bin is available, dig a shallow hole in dirt or sand, and before you start adding concrete, rest the form in the hole, packing it in firmly. Prepare the form and add concrete as described.

The top bin was centred and worked down into the wet concrete. Then a second batch was mixed and shovelled to fill the area around this bin (photograph 8). If you need more, mix more. If you have too much, make a rim that slants up towards the centre. We smoothed the surface with a small trowel (photograph 9). Edge can be rounded with a trowel or an edger. When concrete had set sufficiently to hold its shape, the top dustbin was removed. The concrete was kept damp for three days, while it set. Then the birdbath was removed from the form, placed on a tree stump, and filled with water. It could also be set on rocks or on three pipe legs driven into the ground.

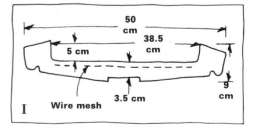

Figure I: Cutaway view of the birdbath shows the wall thickness, the wire-mesh reinforcement, and the space for water.

BIRTHDAY CELEBRATIONS

From Cakes to Games

By Helen Feingold

Celebrating birthdays is a custom in every land. I remember the warmth of birthdays when I was growing up. My Viennese mother, an excellent baker and cook, let us specify the whole day's menus. And there was always a special cake. I have continued the tradition in my own family. When the boys were growing up, I baked, on request, every kind of birthday speciality including cowboy cakes, aeroplane cakes, even battery-lit masterpieces.

In Germany, a birthday party is called *Kinderfeste*, or child's festival. Dressed-up birthday cakes probably evolved from the German custom of serving a butter cake ringed with candles for the birthday child to blow out. The celebrant made a secret wish and believed that if he could extinguish the flames with one giant blow, his wish would come true.

Some historic celebrations

The association of special flowers and precious stones with birth dates has come to us from the East, where birth dates are important because of their relevance in the casting of horoscopes. Birthdays of Eastern rulers were often national holidays—a tradition Europeans adopted in mediaeval times —and were used as occasions for declaring armistices, freeing prisoners, and dispensing alms. Probably the most lavish birthday gift of all times was that given in 1946, on his seventieth birthday, to the Aga Khan by his people, the Khoja Muslims—his weight in diamonds, 110 kilos. The brilliants were valued at nearly £800,000, and an equal sum was distributed to the poor.

Another Eastern birthday party that made a big stir in its time was the one Cleopatra gave for her Roman protector, Mark Antony, shortly before they were defeated by the Roman legions opposing them. At the party, the ill-fated pair gave their guests almost everything they owned, with, says historian Plutarch, "the utmost prodigality of splendour and magnificence so that many guests sat down in want and went home wealthy men".

The luxury of Eastern birthday celebrations spread from Persia and Egypt to Greece and, later, via the Romans, throughout Europe. Eventually, the Church put down the custom as pagan, and by the 14th century, birthdays had become semi-religious and were celebrated on Name Day, sacred to the saint after whom the child had been named. Name Days are still celebrated instead of birth dates in many parts of Europe.

The custom of playing games at parties has more primitive origins. Originally, they were tests of skill, meant to measure the progress of the child during the year past. In the 19th century, dancing and jump rope and badminton were popular party activities.

Today, games are still a highlight of children's parties, and some of those described on pages 80 and 81 make for good fun at adults' parties, too.

Whatever family or national customs you observe at birthday time, there is one tradition you share with everyone in the world—the mood of celebration. A birthday is an event, whether it is fêted by a tennis match, a barbecue, or the giving of a bucketful of diamonds. It will be successful so long as the atmosphere and the trimmings spell out a mood of celebration— the hooray-for-you that is our real gift to the birthday child.

Birthday Stones and Flowers

MONTH	STONE	FLOWER
January	Garnet	Carnation
February	Amethyst	Violet
March	Aquamarine	Jonquil
April	Diamond, sapphire	Daisy
May	Emerald	Lily of the valley
June	Pearl, moonstone	Rose
July	Ruby	Larkspur
August	Cornelian	Gladiolus
September	Sapphire	Aster
October	Opal, beryl	Calendula
November	Topaz	Chrysanthemum
December	Turquoise, ruby	Narcissus

Berry-basket cake is hollowed-out pound cake filled with strawberry cream. Whole strawberries and fresh mint leaves decorate the frosted basket. Recipe on page 75.

1: Select good tools for cake decorating: a pastry bag with an assortment of decorating tips to make borders, flowers, and to write messages; spatulas in several shapes and sizes for preliminary icing; a small wooden spoon for blending icing. Clean your tools well after use and store carefully, so you can find them when you need them.

Kitchen Favourites and Celebrations
The Cake

The real star of any birthday party is the cake. For an adult, you might decorate the cake to suit his tastes or interests. A model-railway fan might enjoy a train decoration. A large needle with flowing thread might be perfect for a sewing enthusiast. For a gardener, decorate with flowers, or make the Berry-Basket Cake pictured on page 73. It is easily made from a mix, as below, or from the Pound Cake recipe on the opposite page.

You will need two packages of pound-cake mix. Or, if you are using the recipe, double all ingredients, and add about 25 minutes to the baking time. Use an ovenproof glass bowl measuring 23 cm in diameter. Grease the inside of the bowl with shortening. Then drop in about a tablespoon of flour; shake the bowl so the inside is covered. Prepare and bake the cake. When it has baked for the prescribed time, test by inserting a knife in the centre. If the cake is done, the knife will come out clean and the cake will be firm to the touch. Let it cool in the bowl for 20 minutes. Then loosen it from the bowl with a flexible spatula; invert it on to a cake rack; turn cake right side up. Allow it to cool. Hollow out the centre with a spoon, leaving a shell 3-cm thick. Reserve the crumbs for the filling. Fill and decorate as in photographs 3, 4, 5.

No matter what theme you choose for decorating the cake, the following recipes will help to ensure success for almost any birthday celebration.

2: Hollow out the bowl-shaped cake, leaving a 3-cm-thick shell. Meanwhile, soak 1 kilo of cleaned and hulled fresh strawberries in kirsch or orange juice.

3: Fill cake shell with crumbled cake mixed with 225 g of double cream, whipped and sweetened with 1 tablespoon icing sugar, and a cup of sliced strawberries.

4: After icing the cake with light-green Butter-cream Icing (see page 77), top it with whole strawberries. The weave of a straw basket is simulated by drawing the tines of a fork across the icing. Garnish with fresh mint leaves.

5: Make the basket handle from a strip of cardboard covered with aluminium foil.

Pound Cake

For an old-fashioned pound cake, use a teaspoon of mace, or lemon, or almond essence, or grated orange rind, or nutmeg instead of vanilla for flavouring.

227 g butter or margarine	5 egg whites, stiffly beaten
184 g sugar	255 g sifted self-raising flour
2 tablespoons lemon juice	$\frac{1}{4}$ teaspoon salt
5 egg yolks	1 teaspoon vanilla essence

Preheat oven to 170 degrees Centigrade, Mark 3. In a large bowl, cream butter until fluffy. Gradually beat in sugar. In a small bowl, combine lemon juice and egg yolks. Beat until thick and lemon-coloured. Stir egg-yolk mixture into butter and sugar. Fold in stiffly beaten egg whites. Sift together flour and salt, and fold into batter. Add vanilla; stir until well blended. Pour into a greased and floured 20 by 12.5 by 7.5 cm bread tin. Bake about 1 hour. Cool in pan 5 minutes, then turn out on to rack.

Yellow Cake

If making cupcakes, use 4 tablespoons batter per cupcake paper or tin.

254 g butter or margarine	1 tablespoon baking powder
280 g sugar	$\frac{1}{4}$ teaspoon salt
6 eggs	1 teaspoon vanilla essence
340 g sifted cake flour	milk

Preheat oven to 180 degrees Centigrade, Mark 4. In a bowl, cream butter until light and fluffy. Add sugar gradually. Beat in eggs one at a time. Then blend in flour, baking powder, salt, vanilla, and finally milk. Spread batter in two greased and floured 23-cm sandwich tins. Bake 30 to 35 minutes, or until cake is firm to touch in centre. Remove from pans; cool; decorate.

Spice Cake

Another birthday stand-by is spice cake, flavoured with treacle.

113 g shortening	$\frac{1}{2}$ teaspoon salt
100 g sugar	1 teaspoon ground cinnamon
1 egg	$\frac{1}{2}$ teaspoon ground ginger
1 cup black treacle	$\frac{1}{2}$ teaspoon ground cloves
283 g sifted all-purpose flour	boiling water
$1\frac{1}{2}$ teaspoons bicarbonate of soda	

Preheat oven to 180 degrees Centigrade, Mark 4. Cream cooking fat and sugar until light and fluffy. Beat in egg; add treacle. Sift together flour, bicarbonate of soda, salt, spices. Alternately add sifted mixture and water, in thirds, to treacle mixture. Bake in two greased and floured, 20- or 23-cm sandwich tins or one 33- by 23- by 5-cm tin, 30 to 35 minutes. When cake is done, rest on cake rack 10 minutes; turn out of pans and let cool.

Variations on a theme

Here are some seasonal suggestions for decorating birthday cakes:

Jan: White-ice spice cake, top with coconut flakes and silver dragees.
Feb: Frost cherry cake white; sprinkle on red sugar; top with cupid.
March: With a leaf tube, make small frosting shamrocks on iced cake.
April: Yellow-frosted yellow cake, white and yellow daisies, green leaves.
May: Circus time coming; decorate with standing animal crackers.
June: Make cupcakes; turn upside down, and ice. Top each with a rose.
July: Make it Fair time with coloured bunting and streamers in frosting.
August, Sept: Make a soccer field with light-green icing, white piping for side lines, and pipe-cleaner goal posts. Pipe on yellow chrysanthemums and falling leaves.
Oct: For Halloween decorate cake with a plain chocolate witch.
Nov: Fireworks; decorate with coloured frosting and metallic dragees.
Dec: Trim like package. Pipe on poinsettias with No. 67 or 74 tube.

This cake celebrates the great occasion with a peppermint-candy border. Ice-cream-cone trees were glazed and sprinkled with green decorating sugar.

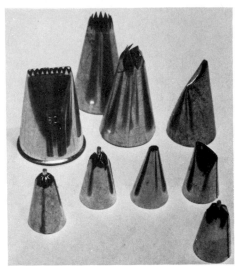

6: Buy pastry decorating tips separately rather than in sets. From bottom left clockwise: No. 67 for leaves; No. 48 for ribbons; No. 21 for large stars; No. 96 for an individual flower; No. 124 for large rose petals and No. 104 for small ones; No. 30 for writing or for eight-point stars; No. 3 for wide scrolls; No. 16 for six-point stars.

Cake decorating

Everyone loves cakes decorated with scrolls and scallops and full-blown red roses. Practising with the wide range of decorating tubes is the basis of cake-decorating skill. There are more than 370 tubes, but professional decorators use only about 20. By varying the pressure when they squeeze icing through the pastry bag, they can create an endless variety of shapes and sizes. Practise first on waxed paper and using plain tubes, numbered from 1 to 12, and writing tubes numbered from 13 to 34. Next, try the leaf tubes, numbered from 65 to 70, ranging from tiny leaves to large ones. By pressing and releasing the icing bag in short spurts or long sweeps, or by changing the angle of the bag or the distance from the cake, you can produce fluted effects, fantasy flowers, swagged borders, swirls, loops, crinkles, and curves. The consistency of the icing is important. If it is hard to force through the tube, add a bit of soft butter. If it flows too easily, it needs more icing sugar.

If you decide to become a cake-decorating expert, you will need several bags—paper, plastic, or canvas—for changes of colour; paste food colours, for richer colour and more variety than liquid colour, and pastry nails to hold cardboard bases for all those still-to-be-created apple blossoms and asters, pink peonies and violets, and flaming red roses in full bloom.

To make the rose-topped cake opposite, use the recipes for Yellow Cake, page 75, and for Butter-cream Icing, page 77. To create the pastry-tube decorations, work with the Flower Icing, page 77. Fill the layers with any fruit preserve. Slicing away the risen centres of the cake layers makes flat surfaces that are easy to work with. To decorate the cake, follow the directions given with the pictures below and on page 77.

7: Gently lower upper layer of cake over filling-topped bottom layer. Stop filling short of edge, so it will not run down side and interfere with icing.

8: Ice side first, using a spatula and a generous amount of icing. Rinse spatula in hot water. Carefully swirl up around side from bottom to top.

9: Use remaining icing for top, making a smooth, sharp edge. For swirled effect on top, use upwards pulling motion. Don't overwork or icing will flatten.

10: Plan a centred design; it is easier than an off-centre one. Make leaf border first; place rose; add leaves around rose. Follow directions on the opposite page.

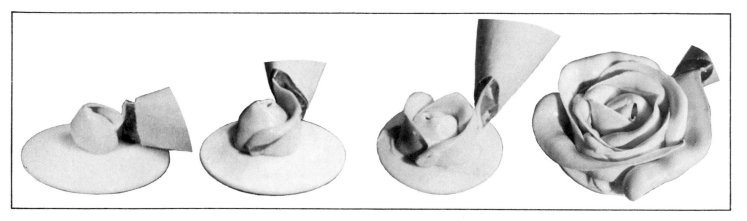

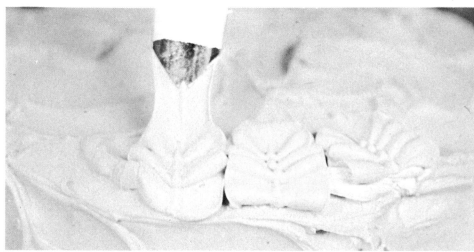

12: Use a large-leaf tube to make the border design, working from edge of cake inwards. With toothpicks, mark inside stopping point for each leaf.

13: Place rose in centre of cake; then form leaves, starting close under rose petals and holding tube almost flat. Chill. Icing tints should be delicate.

▲ 11: To make a rose, centre a mound of icing on a flower nail in centre of a circle of cardboard. Using pastry tip 97, hold bag high and make short strokes to form tight petals. Lower bag for next row. Slant bag out for longer, larger open petals. Chill; peel off cardboard.

For the best-flavoured icing, make Butter Cream. For decorations, try the Flower Icing recipe.

Butter-cream Icing
113 g softened butter of margarine
450 g sifted icing sugar
1½ teaspoons vanilla essence
1 egg white

With electric mixer or wooden spoon, cream butter until fluffy. Slowly add half the sugar, beating it in. Add the vanilla. In another bowl, beat the egg white until foamy. Add to the butter mixture. Add remaining sugar slowly, beating until fluffy. Ice two 20- or 23-cm layers or one 23-cm spring-form or tube cake.

Flower Icing
227 g vegetable cooking fat
½ teaspoon salt
400 g sifted icing sugar
56 g soft butter or margarine
1½ teaspoons vanilla essence

Place cooking fat, salt, and 185 g sugar in electric-mixer bowl. Set mixer at medium speed and mix well. (A wooden spoon may also be used; beat vigorously.) Add one-quarter of the remaining icing sugar; beat; then beat in 1 tablespoon of butter. Repeat three times. Beat until very smooth and easy to spread. Add the vanilla, or substitute 2 teaspoons grated lemon peel or 1 teaspoon almond essence.

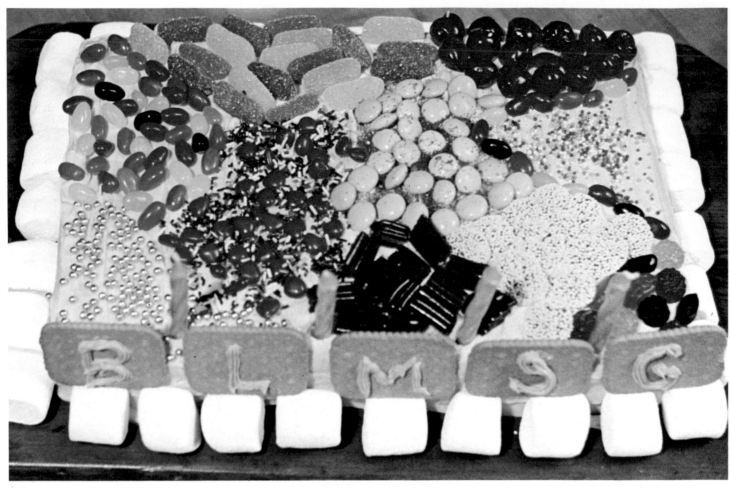

An active imagination made a sugarplum dream come true. The five-year-old originator of this sugary creation called it Patchwork Quilt. Place cards are initialled biscuits.

Kitchen Favourites and Celebrations
For Young Chefs

Half the fun for a birthday child is preparing for the celebration, and nothing pleases him more than helping with the cake. Older children are meticulous about cake decorating. Although younger ones are not skilful enough to do a perfect job, they have such fun they should be encouraged to work with materials they can handle successfully.

The cake pictured above, made from the Yellow Cake recipe on page 75, was decorated by a five-year-old. It may not strike adults as beautiful, but the boy and his guests loved it. Above all, it caused him no frustrations, and he didn't try to do more than he could with a pastry tube or to meet grown-up criteria for a gorgeous birthday cake.

The marshmallow-mounted biscuit place cards were initialled with a No. 16 star tube filled with Butter-cream Icing (page 77). The child practised writing with the tip on the bottom of a pie plate (icing was re-used for the cake) before he initialled the bought vanilla biscuits.

The gumdrop rose on the opposite page looks professional, but can be made by small children. The bud is a rolled-out, rolled-up gumdrop; stem and leaves are rolled-out, shaped gumdrops. It makes a handsome cake-top decoration.

Children like to decorate cupcakes, perhaps because they can be varied and challenge the young decorator's imagination. Use one of the recipes on page 75; bake in bun tins; reduce baking time by about one-quarter.

14: Fit the pastry bag with a No. 16 star tube. Fill with Butter-cream Icing (page 77), and pipe guests' initials on plain biscuits to use for place cards.

15: Dip newly iced cupcakes (Yellow Cake, page 75) in boiled sweets, crushed between sheets of waxed paper with rolling pin. It sparkles and is crunchy.

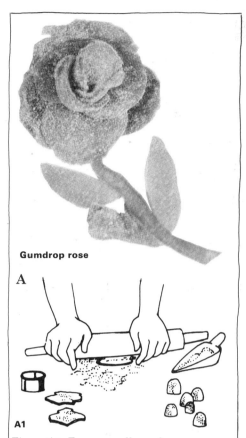

Gumdrop rose

Even toddlers can decorate iced cupcakes successfully. Some garnishes they enjoy working with and that are suitable for borders, patterns, or free-style designs are maraschino cherries, whole or cut up; almonds, slivered, toasted, or finely chopped; gumdrops; sugar-coated chocolate pieces; coconut, tinted or toasted; semisweet-chocolate bits; fresh berries; sugar canes, whole or crushed; animal biscuits; jelly beans.

You will have to do the toasting, chopping, and other such manoeuvring. Offer the artist an assortment of garnishes ready-to-use, piled neatly on squares of waxed paper. Coconut is a favourite. To give it a gala look, put coconut shreds in a small plastic bag; sprinkle with food colour; knead and mix in the bag until the shreds are evenly tinted.

The Yellow Cake recipe, page 75, is almost infallible and a good one for older children to begin with. To vary the flavour, use any of these: 1 teaspoon rum or orange, lemon, almond, or vanilla essence; or 1 teaspoon nutmeg, mace, or cinnamon; or $\frac{1}{2}$ teaspoon allspice; or grated rind of a lemon or orange.

A

Figure A1: For rose, roll gumdrops very thin on sugar-covered board until each is bigger than a 3 cm round cutter.

Figure A2: With cutter, cut the rolled pieces into rounds. Rose above was made with orange, pink, and green gumdrops.

Iced cupcakes for a child's party are decorated with marshmallows, almond flakes, crushed sweets, gumdrops, jellybeans, and the all-important candle.

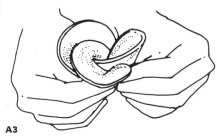

Figure A3: Fit rounds together, pinching at centre until they stick together. Shape petals, curving down outer ones. Trim.

Toys and Games
Birthday-Party Games

Kate Greenaway, nineteenth-century author and illustrator, captured the tradition of game playing at birthday celebrations in her delicate watercolours, some of which are reproduced here. Today's children still look forward to the same party games, and a variety of new ones. With, and even without, modifications, some children's games are good fun at adult parties and help to get things going with a swing.

Every child knows how to play **Musical Chairs,** but a variation called **Musical Bumps** is almost more fun, and chairs are not necessary. The music plays, and when it stops, every child must sit down, anywhere, even on the floor. The last child down is out. The game continues until only one child, the winner, is left.

Balloon Ping-Pong is active but safe for small children. No equipment is required. Line up two teams, of three or four players each, on either side of a bare table about four feet long. Put a balloon in the centre. Teams try to blow it off the opposite side of the table. Score one point for each success; the first side to score five blow-aways wins.

A game enjoyed by children and adults is **O'Grady Says.** In the traditional version, someone volunteers as leader, or O'Grady. He initiates the game by saying, "O'Grady says" and then giving a command and making a gesture. For example, "O'Grady Says rub your stomach and pat your head at the same time". He gestures, and the players imitate him. After several commands, he gives one without the O'Grady Says key. He might say, "Hop on one foot". Anyone who obeys without the key words, O'Grady Says, is out. The game continues until only one player, the winner, remains.

An adult version of O'Grady Says is **O'Grady Asks.** Players answer only questions prefaced by the key words, O'Grady Asks. Questions can be derived from sports, literature, films, or anything that interests the group.

Blindman's Buff, like O'Grady Says, is fun for everyone. Adults in a festive mood enjoy it. It can be played two ways. In both versions, the game is begun by choosing the first Blindman, tying a scarf over his eyes, turning him around and around, and then freeing him to find the other guests. The old-fashioned game requires the Blindman to hunt until he finds someone, who in turn becomes the Blindman. A more recent version requires him to identify the person he has caught by feeling his face and clothes.

Another blindfold game is **Pin the Tail on the Donkey.** In the original game, a picture of a tail-less donkey was taped to the wall. A person, donkey tail in hand, was blindfolded, turned around a few times, and then pointed towards the picture, to pin the tail on it.

Using poster board, felt-tip pens, magazine clippings, string, and a little imagination, Pin the Tail can be given endless variations—for instance, Pin the Heart on the Valentine, the Flea on the Dog.

If the guests need a rest, play **The Fishing Game.** It guarantees that everybody wins. To play it, you need a fishing rod, which could be a stick with a long string tied to one end and an open safety pin attached to the end of the string. You also need a well. To make the well, turn a card table upside down or a coffee table, and wrap the legs with pinned or taped-on brown paper. Fill the well with inexpensive gifts, wrapped and tied with ribbon. Each person has a turn at lowering the hook into the well and catching a prize by hooking the safety pin under a ribbon.

The prizes you select to fill the well are the real fun of the fishing game. They can be gag prizes bought at a novelty shop, or they can be seasonal gifts.

Relay games are popular at birthday parties. A classic, which can be played with small balloons, potatoes, or tissue-paper squares, is the **Soup-spoon Relay.** To play with paper, cut the tissue into 7.5 cm squares, one for each person. Place a pile of squares for each team at one end of the room. At the

Kate Greenaway's tea party.

Playing jump rope.

other end, set two bowls on the floor. When you say Go, the first person on each team must pick up a piece of paper with a teaspoon (no hands) and carry it to his team's bowl. If he drops it, he must pick it up again with the spoon. Once it has been deposited, he runs back, touches his next teammate, and hands him the spoon. The first team to get all the tissues into the bowl wins. You can have paper or balloon relays using plastic drinking straws instead of spoons. The player must hold the paper on the straw by suction while he carries it. Since breath can't be held indefinitely, test yourself to find out how far away to place the bowls.

Some good party games can be played without moving. One is **You Don't Know What You're Talking About.** Each guest must talk for two minutes on an unfamiliar subject. The host makes up subjects in advance. They might include silly ideas, like "A mouse in the Leaning Tower of Pisa". The prize goes to the most ridiculous but most ingenious speech.

Another inactive game is **Ghost.** This takes strategy and accurate spelling. With the guests in a circle, the person who is It says one letter—for instance, s. Every player must have a word in mind when he says a letter. The next person adds a letter—for instance, e. The third person adds another letter. If he chooses e, t, or w, he has completed a word. He becomes the G of Ghost if the completed word was not the one the person who began the word had in mind. He then starts a new word. But if he had chosen n, thinking of the word sent, the round continues. The next person might add an s, thinking of sensational, instead of a t, which would have ended the word. If someone does complete the word correctly, the person who thought of the word gets the G of Ghost. Anyone may be challenged at any time to name the word he has in mind. If his word is not spelled correctly, he loses and collects another letter of Ghost. If his word is right, the challenger gets the letter. The game continues until one person becomes a fully-fledged Ghost. The dictionary is a useful bystander at this game.

For a mixture of the sedate and the rowdy, play **Charade.** One person tries to convey a thought to the rest of the group by acting it out and using sign language. The thought can be a single word, a phrase, a famous saying, or a name. This is a great game for the amateur actors in the group and is usually amusing for the others.

A game that sends guests hustling around the neighbourhood is a **Scavenger Hunt.** The group is divided into two teams, and each is given a list of items to find within a certain time and bring back to the party. Guests are not allowed to buy the items, but must knock on doors and beg or otherwise scavenge. Some of the items should be silly and unusual. The team that finds everything and returns first is the winner.

If you are organizing a birthday celebration during pleasant weather, it is fun to plan the party around a sport. For instance, a tennis or badminton tournament is a happy theme for racket fans, with a barbecue or picnic dinner afterwards. In the winter, take the group for a sleigh ride, and later warm up beside a fire with hot chocolate and toasted marshmallows.

The dancing class.

Badminton.

The illustrations on these pages were taken from the original edition of *Kate Greenaway's Birthday Book for Children*, and are reproduced here by courtesy of the Merrimack Publishing Corporation. Miss Greenaway's children's books won her enormous popularity after the publication in 1878 of her first book of rhymes and pictures, *Under the Window*. Many of her books have been inexpensively reproduced and are again bringing joy to small readers everywhere.

BLOCK PRINTING
Decorative Impressions

By John Noblitt

If you remember your childhood visits to an office and the hours of fun you had playing with the rubber stamps and stamp pads—especially the red-ink one—you will share my enthusiasm for block printing.

With block printing, you can recapture that childhood enjoyment and, at the same time, create designs to decorate useful objects. Rubber stamps are not necessary; simple everyday items can do the job as well. Without investing much time, you can convert potatoes, carrots, gum erasers, and linoleum into very good printing blocks.

The process by which a rubber stamp—and, for that matter, letterpress printing—works is called relief printing, meaning that whatever is raised on the stamp (letters or designs) receives the ink and therefore prints when pressed on a sheet of paper. The method was invented in China in the 10th century. The Chinese used carved blocks of wood as the stamps, originating the technique known today as woodcut printing. The projects described here are a good first step to the more complicated art of making woodcuts, a craft that is described in a later volume.

Block printing lends itself especially to design rather than pictorial representation. Any shape, no matter how irregular, will make an interesting pattern when it is repeated. To get you started, I will show you a few specific designs and how to repeat them; but the real fun of block printing comes when you design and cut your own blocks and see what surprising effects you can achieve.

When printing, work on a hard, flat surface without bumps or ridges. The slightest unevenness in the surface would cause imperfections in your prints. Place sheets of newspaper or brown paper under the printing paper to catch any ink that may bleed through. The weight of the paper advised for each project is determined by its end use—lighter for writing paper, heavier for wallpaper. Rice, newsprint, parchment, and other moderately porous papers are fine for printing. Excessively porous paper will blur the impressions, and shiny, non-porous paper will smear water-based ink.

Graphic Arts
Vegetable Prints

These vegetable-print projects will familiarize you with many of the basic techniques used in all types of block printing.

It's a good idea to select a permanent work area, where you can store your tools (photograph 1), and paper, and leave prints to dry, if necessary.

Potato-print book cover
To make the book cover shown in colour on page 85, you will need two or three large, fresh potatoes; stale ones are not firm enough to produce clear impressions. You will also need a Stanley or mount-cutting knife (see photograph 1); a pre-inked stamp pad in any colour you choose, or a dry stamp pad that you can ink with water-base ink (ordinary writing ink); and a sheet of artist's sketch-pad paper large enough to cover the book.

1: Roller, mount-cutting knife, and gouge with, at its left, U-shape and V-shape blades, for making fine, medium, and broad cuts.

These bold wallpaper patterns were printed with hand-carved linoleum blocks. Directions for producing all of them begin on page 88.

With the exception of the potatoes, all of these can be purchased in an art-supply store. Follow this step-by-step procedure to print the diamond design shown on the book-cover page opposite:

Wash the potato, and cut it in half crosswise with an ordinary kitchen knife. Do not peel it; the skin will provide a good gripping surface.

With a pencil, draw the design exactly as it appears in the pattern, figure A, on the cut end of one of the potato halves.

With the mount-cutting knife, cut away those portions of the potato that correspond to the unshaded areas of the pattern (see photograph 2). Also cut away the excess around the design, so the potato looks like the one in photograph 4. One advantage of working with inexpensive material, such as a vegetable, is that mistakes are not disastrous and can be dealt with easily. Have extra potatoes, in case your first attempts produce some slips, like cutting off a piece of the potato's raised printing area. Always handle the mount-cutting knife carefully to avoid cutting yourself.

Make two or three test prints with your potato by pressing its carved surface on to the stamp pad and then on to paper. You quickly will learn the correct amount of ink and pressure needed to make a good, sharp print. Do not expect perfection; part of the charm of block-printed designs lies in the slight imperfections and irregularities of individual impressions. Notice that the print on the paper is a reverse image of the design on the potato (see photograph 4). This reversal is always the case in printing, and it is vital to keep that in mind as you work.

Draw a small pencil mark on the skin of the potato at a point corresponding to X in figure A. This point will be beside the part of the carved surface that will form the centre of the diamond pattern (see photograph 4) and will be a handy visual reference while you are printing.

Print the pattern's lower-right impression with the X facing upper left.

Rotate the potato 90 degrees, with the pencil mark as the pivot point, and print the second impression.

Print the third and fourth impressions in the same manner, each time rotating 90 degrees around the pivot point. Be sure to ink the potato on the stamp pad for each print. When all four impressions are printed, you should have the completed diamond pattern shown in photograph 4.

Print the entire surface of your paper, repeating the formation of the diamond in the sequence described above. The chance of making a misprint by turning the potato the wrong way are a lot less if you print in the four-print-diamond sequence, rather than in rows. Do not re-ink the stamp pad during the printing of a design. If you did, the impressions made would appear darker than those made earlier. After a five-minute drying period, your brightly patterned paper is ready to become a book cover.

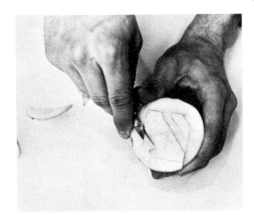

2: Potato as it appears in the process of being carved. Cut along lines of the design to about 6 mm depth, and lift out potato meat that is not to receive ink. Be careful not to cut off the parts of the design that should project.

3: Making the upper-right final print of the diamond pattern. It does not matter which of the four impressions is printed first, as long as you pivot the block around the X on the potato skin as you make each impression.

4: Inked potato and the completed diamond pattern. Cover the paper with horizontal rows of these patterns. Start at upper left of the paper, and work from left to right. Patterns in each row should be directly below those in the row above.

Paper for the book cover shown here was printed with a potato block. Memo pad and envelopes were monogrammed with a carrot-block initial.

Figure A: Design to cut on potato. Shaded areas are the printing (raised) surfaces.

Carrot-print monogrammed memo paper

For this project (see photograph above), you will need a large, fresh carrot, a mount-cutting knife, an inked stamp pad, and a 7.5 by 12.5 cm memo pad. Have an extra carrot or two on hand, in case you make a mistake.

Cut the washed and unpeeled carrot crosswise at its thickest point.

Draw your initial backwards on the cut surface of one of the carrot pieces. Practise this on a piece of paper first, using a mirror to check your drawing for accuracy. Keep the lettering style simple. A fancy letter is a lot more difficult than a block letter to draw in reverse. It is also a good deal harder to carve and mistakes are more obvious.

With the knife, cut around the initial, and cut away the excess carrot surrounding it, so the letter stands up from the surface.

Ink the carrot on the stamp pad, and print the initial at the top centre of a sheet of the memo paper. Do this for every page of the pad, making sure each print is dry before going on to the next. You now have your own personal memo paper to write on.

You might also like to monogram envelopes, like those above, or some stationery. The possibilities are almost endless.

85

Graphic Arts
Eraser Prints

Gum erasers make very good printing blocks. Their rubbery composition is porous enough to absorb the right amount of water-based ink and soft enough to be carved easily. Also, because of its convenient size and shape, a standard gum eraser is a ready-made printing block.

In telling you how to make the design on the paper in the photograph below, I will explain the technique of transferring a drawing to the block and how to work with positive and negative prints.

The materials you will need are a sheet of tracing paper, a sheet of carbon paper, two gum erasers (each measuring approximately 5.5 by 3 by 2 cm), a mat knife, two stamp pads (one inked with blue water-based ink, one with green), and a 60 by 90 cm sheet of parchment-type paper. All of these can be purchased at any art-supply store. I like to have two or three extra erasers and three or four extra sheets of paper, to allow for mistakes in cutting and printing and for experimenting.

B

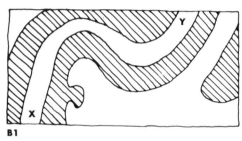

B1

B2

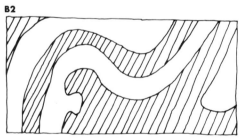

Figure B1: Positive print. B2: Negative. Shading represents inked area of prints.

Diagonal design of this wrapping paper was printed with positive and negative eraser blocks. The same blocks, used on heavier craft paper, made the greeting card.

Transferring a drawing

The first step is to transfer the drawing in figure B1 to the eraser. The method also can be used to transfer a drawing of your own. This is how to proceed with making the block.

Place a sheet of tracing paper over the pattern, figure B1, and trace the design. Place a small sheet of carbon paper on the eraser. Turn the tracing paper over; centre it over the eraser, on the carbon; and transfer the design, as seen through the tracing paper, to the eraser. This design will be a reverse of figure B1, and the print this block produces after it has been carved will look exactly like figure B1.

With the knife and to a depth of no less than 3 mm, carve out the area of the block that corresponds to the unshaded part of the pattern, figure B1. Now complete, this is your positive block.

Making the negative block

To make the negative block from the positive block, follow these steps:

Ink the positive block on the green-ink stamp pad, and print the design on a piece of scrap paper.

Quickly, before the ink dries, firmly press a fresh eraser directly on the still-wet print. Lift off the eraser, and you will see that this green design has now been transferred to the eraser (photograph 5).

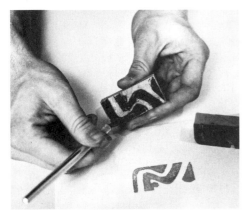

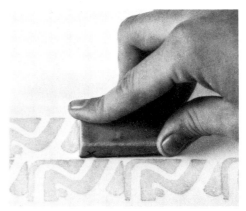

5: Inked areas of negative block are carved away after negative-block design has been made by pressing an eraser on to the still-wet positive-block impression. Technique can be used to make a negative block from a positive of your own design.

6: Positive print, right, and negative are shown here side by side for comparison. Positive green prints and negative blue ones, combined in draughtboard pattern, made the design for the greeting card in the colour photograph opposite.

7: Point just below X on eraser should be lined up with the point on the print, in the row below, that corresponds to Y in figure B1. This will create the design's diagonal effect. Blue overprint from the negative will emphasize this effect.

Carve out the green-covered areas of this second eraser. The raised, uninked areas will be the printing surface, and the print produced will look exactly like the pattern, figure B2. This is your negative block.

Eraser-print wrapping paper

Using green ink on the positive block and blue ink on the negative block, follow this step-by-step procedure:

On the side of the positive block, mark an X at a point corresponding to the X in figure B1.

With the positive block and working across the 60 cm width of the parchment-type paper, print a row of impressions along the bottom of the sheet. Print the remaining rows up from there, one above the other. Ink the block on the pad before making each impression.

Do not line up prints vertically; line up the X on the block with point Y on the print in the row below (see figure B1 and photograph 7).

Along the horizontal rows, when they are dry, print the blue-ink negative block over alternate green prints. Refer to the photograph on the opposite page to make sure you are printing the pattern accurately.

8: Carving the block. Use broad U-gouge blade for carving out an area this large. Cut with saw along line (upper right) to make block perfectly square.

9: Inking the roller. Ink should be of a consistency that covers the roller evenly without being too sticky. If necessary, add linseed oil to thin, but not so much that ink becomes watery. Roller and glass are easily cleaned with mineral spirits.

10: Inking the block. Apply roller several times, rolling it in all directions, until raised surfaces of block are evenly coated with ink. Blocks can be cleaned, stored, and re-used many times.

88

Graphic Arts
Lino Prints

Lino is an ideal printing material. It is soft enough to be carved easily, yet firm enough to produce finely delineated prints. It is especially suitable for printing large designs and covering large surfaces. For easy handling during printing, the lino is usually mounted on blocks of wood or composition board. These lino-mounted blocks are sold in various standard sizes at art-supply stores.

For carving lino, I prefer a tool called a gouge (see photograph 1, page 82). It comes with changeable U- and V-shape blades that make a variety of cuts. Experiment with the blades on a piece of scrap lino or wood, to discover the kind of cut each makes and to learn to manage them with some degree of skill.

Ink is applied to the lino with a special roller (see photograph 1, page 82). It looks and works like a small paint roller, but is used to apply ink rather than paint.

Oil-base ink works best for lino printing. It is sold in tubes and, like oil paint, can be thinned, if necessary, with linseed oil. Unlike water-based ink, it is indelible after a somewhat long (overnight) drying period. Water-based ink dries in a few minutes.

I prefer glass for inking the roller (photograph 9), because it has a smooth, hard surface and can be cleaned easily. However, if glass is not available, you can substitute the smooth side of some scrap lino.

It is possible to print on a variety of surfaces with oil-based ink. In addition to the types of porous paper mentioned in the preceding projects, this ink can be printed on glossy paper or natural-fibre fabrics with good results. A smooth fabric surface is best.

Best for printing are all-cotton fabrics or blends that are mostly cotton. Synthetic fabrics do not take ink as well. Always use indelible oil-based ink on fabrics. Before printing, wash the fabric to remove any sizing that may have been applied to it.

Make small samples of each of the patterns described below before undertaking to print enough paper to use as a wall covering. You will then be in a better position to select the pattern you like best.

Chevron-pattern wallpaper
To make the chevron print shown on the top sample of wallpaper in the

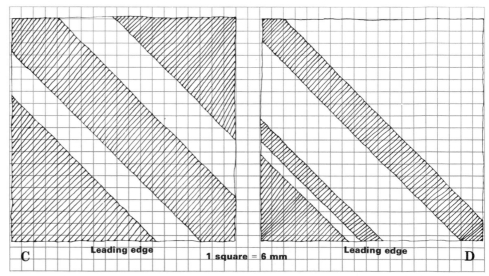

Figure C: Pattern for making red block. Use grid to enlarge it to 12.5 cm square.

Figure D: Pattern for making yellow block. Use thin V-gouge blade to cut fine line.

This table setting includes fabric napkins that were block printed. Designs like this can be applied to curtains, tablecloths, or fabric for a dress or caftan.

Design was made by printing a single unit of pattern described on following page.

photograph on page 83, you will need a 12.5-by-17.5 cm lino block, as sold in art-supply shops, for printing; a gouge (see photograph 1, page 82); a tube of red oil-based ink; linseed oil; a small panel of glass (photograph 9); a roller (see photograph 1); heavyweight craft paper in 90-cm wide rolls. You will need enough rolls to cover the wall or walls of the room you plan to wallpaper. All these materials are available at art-supply shops. Here is the step-by-step procedure:

Saw off 5 cm of the rectangular lino block, pictured in photograph 8, to make it a 12.5 by 12.5 cm square.

With a pencil, draw a grid of 6 mm squares on the block's light-coloured surface. Then draw on the block the design shown in the pattern, figure C, referring to the Craftnote on page 129 for directions for enlarging and transferring a design on a grid.

With the gouge, carve the lino to a depth of no less than 3 mm in the areas corresponding to the white areas of the pattern, figure C. Carving removes the lino's light-coloured top veneer and exposes the darker layer underneath. This contrast makes it easy to keep track of your work, because it so clearly defines carved and uncarved areas.

11: For making the chevron pattern, print the first square of the pattern with the arrow on the back of the block pointing up. Press the block firmly with both hands. Then carefully lift it straight up, so that it does not move on the paper and smear the impression.

12: Ink the block again with the roller, and with the arrow pointing to the right, print the second square beside the first. Visually align the edge of the block with the edge of the previous print.

13: Here is the completed chevron pattern basic to the large chevron wallpaper design. The block used for this can be worked in many different ways to originate other designs. Alternating herring-bone rows of red and blue, for instance, creates a design reminiscent of North American Indian blanket motifs.

14: Printing the last yellow square on the red diamond pattern. Notice direction of the arrow. The yellow overprint on the red produces red, white, and orange. You must be sure the red ink is dry before you print with the yellow ink.

Squeeze out about a toothpaste squeeze of the oil-based ink on to the centre of the glass panel.

Ink the roller by rolling it three or four times in one direction in the ink, or until it is evenly covered (photograph 9, page 88). The ink should be tacky, but not liquid. If it ripples when rolled with the roller, it is too thick and should be thinned with linseed oil.

Roll the roller across the carved surface of the block, to apply the ink evenly (photograph 10, page 88). Only the ungouged surfaces should receive ink. Be careful not to use too much, or it will run into the gouged areas. The block must be reinked each time you print.

Make two or three prints by turning the block over and pressing it firmly and with even pressure on a piece of scrap paper. Notice that the printed design is a reverse image of the design on the block.

Draw an arrow on the back of the block pointing to the block's leading edge (see pattern, figure C, page 88). This is done to provide a clear reference point when I describe the positions of the block which are necessary to execute the patterns.

Print the first square in the paper's upper left corner, with the arrow on the back of the block pointing up (photograph 11).

Print the second square to the right of the first, with the arrow on the back of the block pointing to the right (photograph 12). The completed design should appear as it does in photograph 13.

Repeat this chevron design side by side across the width of the paper, and print identical rows—one directly below the other—down the length of the paper. As you work, refer to the photograph on page 83, to be sure you are printing the pattern accurately.

Diamond-pattern wallpaper

The diamond print shown on the centre sample of wallpaper in the photograph on page 83 is a two-colour pattern that uses the red-ink block of the chevron design and a second block, to be inked with yellow. Follow this step-by-step procedure to achieve the diamond pattern:

With the red block, print the two squares of the chevron pattern, as previously described (see photographs 11 and 12).

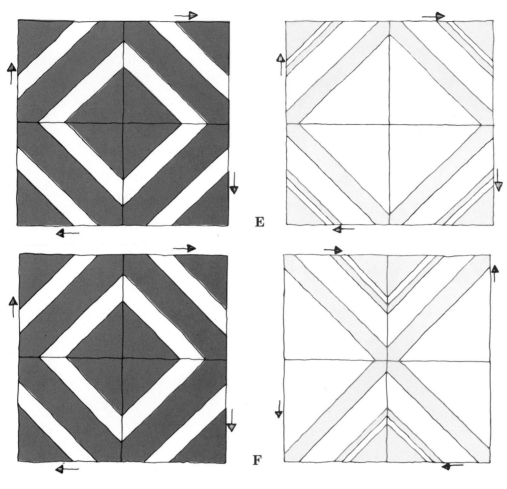

E

F

◀ Figure E: Completed red diamond pattern. The arrows show proper position of the arrow on the back of the block as each square is printed. Right, the completed yellow diamond pattern. This design printed over the red makes the red-white-and-orange diamond-pattern wallpaper, page 83. The yellow could be alternated with the red, draughtboard style, to make a very different pattern.

◀ Figure F: Red block is printed exactly the same for both diamond and plaid wallpapers. But the yellow block is printed differently. Right, the completed yellow pattern for the plaid-pattern wallpaper. By aligning the arrow on the back of the yellow block with the arrows shown, this new design is created.

After printing the second square, turn the block 90 degrees, so the arrow on the back of the block points down, and print the third square directly below the second (see the pattern at left in figure E).

Print the fourth and last square by again turning the block 90 degrees, so the arrow is pointing to the left. The completed red diamond should appear as it does in figure E, left.

Cover all areas of the paper, repeating the diamond-pattern sequence described above. Let dry overnight.

To prepare the roller and glass to receive ink of a different colour, clean them with mineral spirits, turpentine, or a similar paint solvent.

Carve the block that is to be inked with yellow, following the directions for making the red block, but using the pattern shown in figure D, page 88. On the back of the block, mark an arrow pointing to the leading edge indicated in figure D.

After making sure the red ink you printed the day before is thoroughly dry, print the yellow block in a diamond pattern (see pattern at the right in figure E) directly over one of the red diamond patterns already printed (photograph 14). Be sure the arrow on the block's back follows those in figure E. Cover all red diamonds with yellow in this manner.

Plaid-pattern wallpaper
To make the plaid print shown in the photograph on page 83, follow all the steps described above for printing the red diamond pattern; but follow the diagram and arrows of figure F, right, for printing the yellow. The design that results from this overprint is shown in figure G.

G

Figure G: This shows the design printed with the yellow block (figure F, right) superimposed on the red design (figure F, left). This is what the four-square unit of the plaid design should look like. Yellow lines cut diagonally across red lines. Repeating these units, one immediately beside the other, creates an overall plaid-like pattern. See the photograph on page 83.

BONSAI
Dwarfed Trees

By Marcial Rodriguez-Brossoise

Bonsai is a wonderfully refined art that deals with nature in miniature. The word means "tray arrangement" in Japanese. If you look at some examples, you will see they are just that: miniature trees or woody shrubs planted in a traylike container and trained, by wiring, pruning, and root cutting, to look exactly like great old trees—elms or junipers, for instance. Every bonsai imitates a setting in nature, and looking at one is like viewing a fragment of a country scene from a distant vantage point. Some bonsai are quite gnarled and twisted and appear to have withstood all of nature's hardships. And they have—not from the effects of rock, sand, and wind, but under the patient care of a gardener-artist who has controlled their growth for many years.

Originating in China more than 2,000 years ago, the art of bonsai was refined and developed in Japan; Japanese enthusiasts passed on age-old specimens from one generation to the next. Many of these priceless bonsai were lost during World War II, and the art itself declined. But it has flourished again in Japan at the same time as it has come to popularity in the West.

Bonsai's appeal lies in the way it presents the beauties of nature in a microcosm. Look at an elm bonsai, standing a few feet from it. If it were a mature, natural elm, you would have to be 90 metres or more away to get the same effect. And, as a hobby and craft, bonsai derives much of its popularity from the way what was once a centuries-long process can, today, be handled in a relatively short time.

To try your hand at bonsai, you can find a suitable plant in the wild, or growing in a container at your local nursery. The primary thing to keep in mind is that a plant suffers some degree of shock when it is moved, transplanted, or pruned. Therefore, you must take one step at a time and allow the plant to recover between moves. If you transplant from the natural state, let your tree or shrub grow until it is well adapted to a pot. Then transfer it to a smaller container—not necessarily a bonsai tray, just a smaller pot. From that point on, wiring, pruning, and root cutting must be done carefully and a little at a time. Reduce the number of branches in about the same proportion as the root reduction, but don't remove any branches necessary to the overall branch framework you are aiming for. Don't transfer a plant from a nursery container to a bonsai pot, remove some branches, and wire the rest, all in one day. It might look pretty for a week and then die.

If you become involved in bonsai, it's a good idea to begin a collection of containers in different sizes and colours, from which to choose. Keep them on a shelf in your work area, so you can see what you have. Containers vary from small inexpensive pots to nearly priceless pieces of china. Also, assemble the necessary tools (see photograph 1, page 94). Kits of bonsai tools from Japan are available, or you can improvise with similar tools found in most kitchens and workshops. A kitchen fork, for example, can be substituted for the chopstick or dowel used to remove soil from the plant's root ball and to work new soil in and around the roots when the tree is replanted in its new container.

This driftwood-style bonsai is a juniper (*Juniperus virginiana*, Western red-cedar). It is the subject of the first project, beginning on page 95. With your hand, block out the container: is the tree 30 cm or 3.5 m tall? Actually, it is a 30 cm tree that appears to have struggled for survival on a rocky, wind-swept cliff.

Trees and Shrubs for Bonsai

FLOWERING

Cercis canadensis—Eastern redbud
Chaenomeles japonica—Japanese quince
Cotoneaster microphylla thymifolia—Thyme rockspray
Lagerstroemia indica—Crape-myrtle
Magnolia kobus—Magnolia
Malus floribunda—Japanese crab apple
Prunus serrulata—Flowering cherry

TROPICAL

Bougainvillea—'Barbara Karst'
Carissa grandiflora—Natal-plum
Citrus mitis—Calamondin
Cuphea hyssopifolia—False heather
Ficus diversifolia—Mistletoe fig
Gardenia thunbergia—Gardenia
Jacaranda acutifolia—Mimosa-leaved Jacaranda
Malpighia coccigera—Holly malpighia
Myrtus communis—Myrtle
Punica granatum var. *nana*—Dwarf pomegranate
Schinus molle—Peppertree

DECIDUOUS

Acer buergerianum—Trident maple
Acer palmatum—Japanese maple
Ginkgo biloba—Maidenhair-tree
Liquidambar styraciflua—Sweet gum
Quercus ilicifolia—Scrub oak
Ulmus crassifolia—Cedar elm
Ulmus parvifolia—Chinese elm
Zelkova serrata—Zelkova

EVERGREEN (BROADLEAF AND NEEDLE)

Buxus microphylla japonica—
    Japanese little-leaf boxwood
Cedrus atlantica—Atlas cedar
Chamaecyparis obtusa—Hinoki-cypress
Chamaecyparis pisifera—Sawara cypress
Cotoneaster horizontalis—Rockspray
Hedera helix—English ivy
Ilex pernyi—Perny holly
Juniperus chinensis—Chinese juniper
Juniperus osteosperma—Utah juniper
Juniperus virginiana—Western red-cedar
Kalmia angustifolia—Sheep-laurel
Pinus banksiana—Jack pine
Pinus mugo—Mugho pine
Pyracantha coccinea cultivars—Firethorn
Tsuga canadensis pendula—
    Sargent's weeping hemlock

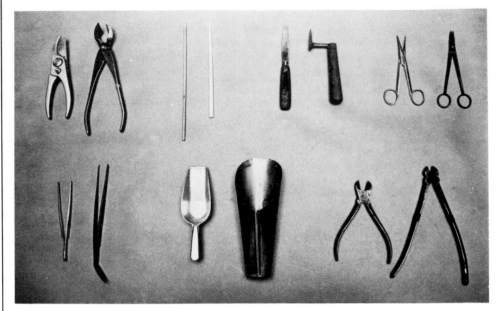

1: Basic bonsai tools shown in pairs. European version always on the left and Japanese on the right. Upper row, left to right: pruning shears, sharpened dowel (chopstick), palette knife, and short-bladed scissors. Lower row, left to right: long tweezers, kitchen scoop, and pincers (wire cutters).

Potting soil for bonsai can be purchased at some nurseries, or you can mix your own. There are many variations of bonsai soils, not the least of which is geographical; but the three basic ingredients are clay, sand, and humus. The clay is for moisture retention, the sand for drainage, and the humus for nutrients. To prepare such a growing medium, you must be able to recognize soil types and be equipped to screen and mix them. For that reason, you may be wise to take advantage of the bagged potting soil available in most local garden centres. Or if you have access to reasonably good garden loam—in which you can grow healthy geraniums, for instance— you can mix it in equal proportions with sphagnum peat moss and coarse Perlite. If you purchase pre-mixed potting soil, be sure it does not contain timed-release fertilizer pellets, because they tend to promote growth that is too rapid for bonsai training.

If you are reasonably successful as a gardener, the transition to bonsai will not be difficult. However, the art of bonsai often appeals to people who have never before gardened. Whether you belong in the first or the second category, a review of plant physiology will be helpful. Plants live and grow by means of two basic chemical processes—respiration and photosynthesis. In the process of respiration, the organic food a plant absorbs is turned into building material, with carbon dioxide and water as by-products. The process of photosynthesis—in the presence of sunlight and with the plant's chlorophyll acting as a catalyst—takes this carbon dioxide and water and turns them into a sugar called glucose. Obviously, if you deprive a plant of any or all of the food and water it needs for healthy growth, these physiological processes will be interrupted to a certain extent, and the plant will grow at a much slower rate or hardly at all. This is basically—together with root and branch pruning—how the stunting of a bonsai is achieved.

The projects that follow are designed to acquaint you with the basic techniques of bonsai and allow you to experiment with and learn this contemporary garden-art form. Involvement in bonsai may lead you to membership in a local or national bonsai organization, to classes with one of the Japanese bonsai masters, and possibly to ownership of an ancient—and very valuable—bonsai specimen purchased at an auction.

Greenery and Growing Things
Driftwood Bonsai

This first of our plantings is quite complicated—but for a purpose. It introduces most of the basic techniques you need for any bonsai project. To get started on it, you will need the following: A stunted plant purchased from a nursery or gathered in the wild (I found the naturally stunted specimen of Western red-cedar, *Juniperus virginiana*, shown in the photograph on page 92, in an abandoned field); the tools in photograph 1, plus a small artist's brush; two or three food-storage plastic bags and some twine; a standard clay or plastic pot, big enough for the plant's root ball; a bonsai container and enough bonsai soil to fill it; enough aluminium or plastic mesh screening to cover the drainage holes in the bottom of the container, and some masking tape (see figure A); medium-gauge wire to hold the plant in place and some 12- to 24-gauge wire to use in training the branches (see photograph 10, page 97); enough woods moss to cover the soil in the bonsai container. Keep in mind that you must have the property owner's permission when you dig plants in the wild.

The step-by-step photographs used here were taken in a relatively short period of time for the sake of instruction. In practice, these steps may occur days, weeks, or even months apart.

This is the procedure: Dig up your specimen, preserving as much of the root structure as possible. Cover the root ball with a plastic bag, secured with twine (photograph 2); tie another bag over the branches. This keeps the

2: This 30-cm tall Western red cedar was dug from a hayfield. It had been mowed over many times, which gave it the stunted appearance of a bonsai.

3: The tree potted in its first container. It must remain here, in subdued light, until it has survived transplanting and is accustomed to container living.

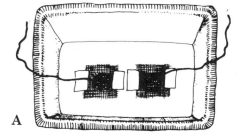

A

Figure A: Looking into tray container. Drainage holes are covered with mesh squares secured with tape. Attached through mesh and holes are lengths of medium-gauge wire to hold tree in place.

roots and branches moist and prevents damage before the plant is potted.

At home, put the plant in a standard clay or plastic pot, and fill with soil (photograph 3). Water well, so the entire root ball and the new soil are thoroughly moistened. When the plant is established in its pot—that is, has recovered from transplanting—it will be ready to be put into a bonsai container of suitable shape, size and colour. Some plants recover quickly and show signs of healthy new growth in three or four weeks. Others may remain in a state of semidormancy for several months before they show signs of new life and are ready to be transplanted.

Unpot the plant; shake excess soil from the root system; pick away compacted soil with a dowel or chopstick (photograph 4). The roots will be clearly visible, and you can prune back enough of them to allow the plant to sit comfortably in the shallow bonsai container.

Cut two squares of aluminium or plastic mesh, to cover the container's two drainage holes. Secure them in place with masking tape, and insert a 61-cm length of medium-gauge wire up through each of the drainage holes and mesh squares (figure A, page 95). The screening will keep the soil from washing out, and the wire will anchor the plant.

Place about 1.5 cm of soil in the container, and position the tree. (Traditionally, a bonsai is placed off-centre.) Turn it and view it from all angles until you decide which is the most attractive side to face front. Studying pictures of bonsai and visiting public gardens where bonsai are displayed will help you get a feeling for the special look of a bonsai. What you should strive for, ultimately, is a replica in miniature of a full grown tree.

Wire the tree in place by crossing the anchor wires over the roots and twisting the ends together (photograph 5). Cut off the excess wire, and press the twisted ends into the soil or root ball.

Add soil up to the container's lip, working it in and around the root mass with the wooden dowel or chopstick (photograph 6). This eliminates air pockets and brings the soil into close contact with the roots. Firm the soil with your fingers or the palette knife (photograph 7). Don't smooth the surface, however; leave some irregularities, to suggest natural valleys and hills in a landscape.

Expose parts of the heavy roots at the base of the tree trunk by brushing away a little of the soil with the artist's brush. This gives the tree a solid-looking base and a semblance of age.

Water gently with a shower-type watering can or a syringe—(not a strong stream, nor a mist).

Place moss on the soil. Don't use the coarse-textured moss sold by florists, but the velvety kind that grows in moist, shaded places in the woods. When you collect it, put in a plastic bag with a little water to keep it fresh. Before applying it to the bonsai, soak it in a small

Instructions for planting a driftwood-style bonsai like this one begin on page 95. The container complements the tree the way a frame does a picture.

4: Removing the old soil from the roots. After the soil is removed, the root mass must be reduced by pruning, so it will fit into the shallow bonsai container.

5: Securing the tree in place with wire. Twist the root mass gently into the first 1.5 cm layer of soil, and then wrap the wire, to hold it firmly.

6: Working soil around the roots with the chopstick. This technique prevents air pockets, thus ensuring the least possible transplanting shock to roots.

7: Firming the soil with a palette knife. Making little valleys and hills in the soil will provide a more realistically natural setting for your tree.

8: Trimming unwanted branches as bonsai is shaped. Tweezers can be used to remove dead needles. Tree will be healthier if some live branches are also removed.

9: Trimming away part of outer layer of bark. In order not to endanger the tree's life, trim only a small area at a time, preferably several weeks apart.

10: Assorted wires, ranging in gauge from 12 to 24. These are necessary to hold the tree in place and to train branches to conform to your design conception.

11: Wiring a branch—with the bonsai placed on a turntable (see figure B). Wire should be one-quarter the diameter of the branch and one-third longer.

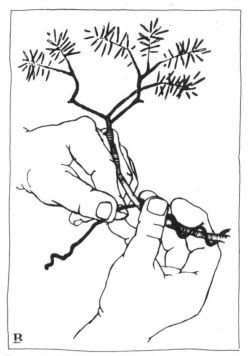

Figure B: To train a branch, wind the wire corkscrew-style along its length. Cut off excess wire, and bend branch to desired position. After several months, when the branch will remain in position by itself, wire can be removed. Also remove wire if it seems to be cutting into the bark.

bowl of water (see photograph 14, page 98). After the moss has been applied, clean it of any dried or extraneous material with tweezers. A pair of tweezers is the bonsai artist's rake.

With scissors, trim any dead leaves or unwanted branches from the tree (photograph 8). Try to emphasize the structural framework of the branches. Study the tree carefully before you cut off anything. You can block out a questionable branch with your hand, to see the effect of its removal, or you can slip a piece of white paper around it and step back to get a better perspective. Leave some dead branches, and peel away their bark to emphasize the driftwood look.

It is a good idea, at this stage of a bonsai preparation, to place the container and plant on some sort of turntable (see photograph 11). This lets you have immediate access to all sides of a plant. You can make a turntable, or use a potter's wheel, or no-longer functioning record player.

Peel away the trunk's outer layer of bark with a knife (photograph 9), to further emphasize the weather-beaten appearance. Do this over an extended period, peeling only small sections of bark at a time. In that way, you will not endanger the tree's life.

To set and train a living branch to any position you like, coil a length of light wire around it (photograph 11 and figure B), and bend the wire, with the branch, to the desired setting. The diameter of the wire should be roughly one-quarter that of the branch to be trained.

If you follow all these steps and apply lots of devotion, this pretty little tree will prosper and become a bonsai of subtle mood and beauty. Read as many books as you can on the subject, and examine trees and shrubs in their natural settings, with an eye towards capturing their beauty in your work. In this way, you will keep on developing as a bonsai artist.

12: An unprepossessing dwarf pomegranate before it was shaped to become a bonsai.

13: Clipping branches and dead twigs. This is done to thin the plant and give it a starker and more interesting silhouette.

14: Adding woods moss to the soil surface. The moss is soaked in a small bowl of water before it is applied to the bonsai.

15: Wiring the branches. Ideally, this should not be done until the bonsai has become established in its new container.

Greenery and Growing Things
Tropical Bonsai

The bonsai look can be achieved almost overnight by working with nursery stock that is stunted. The dwarf pomegranate (*Punica granatum* var. *nana*) I purchased for this project would never win a prize for symmetry; but it was healthy, and its distressed appearance made it look a good bonsai subject (photograph 12). Look for such less-than-perfect specimens at your nursery. You will find many, and they are often available at reduced prices.

Flowering tropical plants cannot be authentic bonsai, because they are not long-lived, as must be true bonsai plants such as the non-tropical junipers and zelkovas. However, their decorative foliage and flowers make them acceptable to all but a purist as simulated bonsai. Choose only plants with small flowers; those with large blossoms, such as *Magnolia grandiflora* and Chinese hibiscus, are unsuited for the miniature setting that creates the bonsai illusion. Consult the list on page 94 for suitable tropicals.

To plant this bonsai, you will need all the tools and materials used for the previous project. Follow this procedure:

Clip off all dead twigs and crossing branches (photograph 13), to give a more sparse and artistically clean look. Decide whether any others should go. If in doubt, leave them until you are sure cutting is the right move. Pruning is easy, mistakes impossible to correct.

Remove the plant from its pot; prepare the roots; plant it in a suitable bonsai container; add woods moss (photograph 14). For all these steps, follow the directions given for the first project.

Cut away more branches, and wire the rest, to mould them into interesting lines (photograph 15). This step of cutting and wiring might well be postponed until a few weeks after the planting is done.

Your completed dwarf-pomegranate "bonsai" will make an excellent house plant. It will thrive near a sunny window in a town flat, and will grow well under fluorescent light. Be careful to water it often enough to keep the soil moist at all times. Shallow containers dry out quickly.

This dwarf pomegranate is one of the tropical flowering plants that make excellent pseudo-bonsai. Its small leaves and flowers are well suited to miniaturization.

Greenery and Growing Things
Cascade Bonsai

A cascade-style bonsai is a plant trained to grow over and down the side of its container. A deeper container than the tray type is desirable since it balances the cascade effect.

The *Juniperus pro cumbens mana*, a needle evergreen I used for this project, was bought from a nursery (photograph 16). An experienced bonsai artist could prepare it in a matter of hours. However, it would be better, if you are a beginner, to achieve the same effect over a period of months, or even years—cutting and shaping the plant a little at a time.

Using materials and tools described previously, follow this procedure:

Remove the plant from its container, and clip off extraneous branches (photograph 17). Some may be dead; others may obscure handsome growth patterns. Remove dead needles with tweezers.

Brush away some of the soil, to expose the trunk, and to determine the placement of large roots joined to the trunk. Tops of these will be exposed.

Prepare the roots as directed for the first project.

Prepare the wire anchors for the roots by twisting a length of medium-gauge wire at its middle around a small piece of heavier wire and inserting the two ends through the drainage hole in the bottom of the container (see figure C). These wires will secure the root ball.

Position the tree in the bonsai pot (photograph 19).

Fasten the roots, and add soil and moss as in preceding projects.

This *Chamaecyparis* evergreen has been pruned and potted to form a traditional cascade-style bonsai. The type is best displayed on a pedestal or shelf.

16: The evergreen in its original container at the nursery. It already shows signs of being a likely candidate for the cascade style of bonsai.

17: Clipping some branches to reveal the plant's most pleasing lines. This pruning is most safely done little by little over a period of several months.

18: Removing soil from trunk and adjoining large roots with a basting brush. Or use an artist's brush. Leave top of large trunk roots exposed.

19: Positioning the plant to determine the best angle and height. Cascading end eventually should be wired and trained to grow well below the container's bottom.

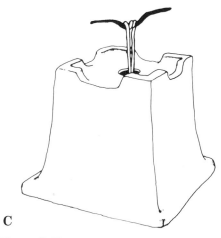

C

Figure C: The cascade pot upside down, to show how wires that will hold plant in place extend through the drainage holes and are secured underneath the pot.

Rock-Grown Bonsai

These Japanese-maple seedlings, growing from a rock as if by magic, represent another traditional kind of bonsai—the rock-grown variety. As they are in shallow soil, they require frequent watering.

A rock-grown bonsai is planted on or in a rock, the rock taking the place of a container. Again, we are imitating nature—in this case, those rare, but charming, instances when trees or shrubs grow from large rock outcroppings and crevices.

You will need, beside the tools and materials described on pages 94 and 95, a rock whose size is in proportion to that of your plant. For the rock planting pictured here, I selected six colourful Japanese-maple seedlings; but any small-leaved, deciduous tree or shrub will do. Here is the procedure for creating a rock-grown bonsai.

Decide on the most pleasing arrangement of rock and plant or plants (photograph 21). A natural crevice or hollow in the rock provides the most suitable area for planting.

To hold the plant's roots in place, secure lengths of wire around the rock. Remove when the roots have become established.

Put a thin layer of wet soil on the rock; press the roots of the plants into it (photograph 22), and secure them with the wires.

Add more wet soil, to cover the roots, and then woods moss (photograph 23).

This kind of bonsai demands more exacting care and attention than any other. The small amount of soil will dry out not only overnight, but literally every few hours in very hot, dry weather. So water often.

20: The six seedlings in their original containers. Notice the variety of shapes among them. Any deciduous, small-leaved plant is suitable for rock-grown bonsai.

21: Arranging the plants on the rock. Decide on the most unusual, yet natural grouping. Multiple plants are not necessary; one can be just as effective.

22: Planting the trees in an existing crevice in the rock. It is most important, because of the small amount of soil, that the plants be firmly secured with wire.

23: Adding woods moss. Notice how plants fan out. As they grow, they can be trained to look like a tranquil grove of trees or a single, multiple-stalk shrub.

Greenery and Growing Things
Miniature Bonsai

Traditional super-small bonsai, called "mame" in Japanese, are a wonderfully artistic way of planting and displaying tiny plants. The miniature in this project is a specimen of *Ulmus parvifolia*, a small-leaved elm I had grown for two years from a cutting (photograph 24).

The techniques for planting this bonsai are much the same as those described earlier. Special considerations arise only from the small-scale nature of the work, akin to the demands of other fine-detail crafts, such as miniature oil painting and miniature flower arranging. As does any miniature, a tiny bonsai requires a steady hand and a good eye, but the value and charm of the finished product are heightened by its diminutive size. Proceed as follows:

Prepare the container with tape, mesh, and wire, as in photograph 24.

24: *Ulmus parvifolia* and bonsai container. A suitably shaped ashtray, with drainage hole drilled in bottom, could substitute.

The 30-cm long turtle in this picture gives an idea of how tiny the elm bonsai is. This delicate bonsai is simple to plant and trim to an appealing shape.

25: Snipping excess roots. Also remove most of the soil from around the roots with a chopstick or sharpened dowel.

26: Adding soil. When you work in so small a space, it is especially important to make sure soil contacts all roots.

Remove the plant from its original container, and clip off excess roots with scissors (photograph 25).

Position the little tree in the bonsai container, and wire the roots. Clip superfluous wire, and hide the twisted ends among the roots.

With the kitchen scoop, slide some soil into the container; then work it closely around the roots with the chopstick (photograph 26).

Add woods moss to soil surface. Tweezers are especially useful for this.

Trim off twigs, to shape the plant into a pleasant form (photograph 27). Do not leave stubs; always cut cleanly to the branch. Use a sharp knife or scissors so the back is not peeled or torn away. Any work of this sort must be done very carefully, so as not to endanger the plant's life.

Display your completed miniature bonsai on a table or shelf, along with treasured curios and artifacts. Be sure it receives plenty of light.

27: Clipping twigs to shape the tiny tree. This must be done gradually, or the delicate seedling will be damaged.

BOOKBINDING
Recover Old Favourites

By Richard Minsky

A book is bound when the leaves of paper have been folded, collected in order, and fastened together within a protective cover. The ancestor of today's book is the second-century Roman codex, which consisted of separate pages fastened at one edge. Until that time, writings had been inscribed on long rolls of papyrus or parchment, as was done by the early Egyptians and Greeks. The newer, more compact form gained popularity, and by the 16th century bookbinding had evolved into a specialized craft, combining the skills of papermaker, printer, weaver, leatherworker, and goldsmith. Today, there are computerized machines capable of binding hundreds of books per minute. Machine-bound books are inexpensive. Though not as strong, durable, or beautiful as handbound volumes, they serve the purposes of our fast-paced world. Hand binding is now reserved for those special books we wish to treasure. It is time-consuming and requires expertise, but it rewards its practitioners with supremely beautiful results.

Tools and materials

For bookbinding you will need some items of equipment including tools and in acquiring these it is better not to over-economise. If your work is to have quality, then the tools you use must have it too.

The tools and materials listed below are basic supplies which are a "must" for amateur bookbinders.

Awl: Used to pierce holes in cover boards for lacing in cords.

Backing boards: Two wedge-shaped hardwood boards with bevelled top edge, to place at the sides of a book while it is being backed. See figure G and photographs 16 and 17 on pages 110 and 111.

Beeswax: Used to lubricate thread during sewing and to waterproof the top edge of the book after the edge is painted.

Binder's cord: Two- or three-strand linen cord is best for binding.

Binder's thread: No. 30 French linen thread is best for sewing sections.

Bone folder: Smooth, knife-shaped tool, made of plastic, wood, or bone. Used to crease smoothly and to burnish. See photograph 4 on page 106.

Brushes: Round brushes, in assorted sizes. Used to apply glue and paste.

Finishing tools: Various hand tools used in the decoration of leather covers, each designed to produce a distinct motif when heated and hand pressed into dampened leather.

Glue: Polyvinyl acetate (PVA).

Hacksaw blade: Used to cut shallow grooves in backbone to fit cords.

Hammer: A cobbler's hammer, with a broad, flat face, is the best, but a household hammer may be used.

Sixteenth-century Venetian engraving used to publicise newly bound editions.

Handbound diary, with leather of one colour inset into another and tooling of gold foil, is a project for the more ambitious student binder. See page 108.

1: The basic tools of the bookbinder. From left to right, top row (tools on paring stone): Sponge, hammer, skiving knife, scalpel, paring knife, spring dividers, binder's cord and thread, beeswax, awl, mount-cutting knife, glue, brushes. Bottom row: try-square, steel ruler, hacksaw blade, shears, small thin square of metal, and, below glue jar, two bone folders, smaller one with pointed end.

Mount-cutting knife: Used for precise cutting of paper and cover boards.

Paring knife: Several types of knife are used to pare down the suede side of leather where it will be shaped to the book.

Paring stone: Heavy, flat piece of smooth stone, against which the leather can be pared down. Marble is preferred.

Pressing boards: Two flat wooden boards to place at the sides of a book when it is clamped in a press or vice. Shown throughout both projects, but most clearly in photograph 11, page 107.

Scalpel: For delicate cutting. Blade must be thin and sharp. A thin carving blade in a holder may be used in place of a scalpel.

Shears: For cutting cloth and thread. Any sharp pair will do.

Skiving knife: Curved knife used in the paring down of the suede side of leather.

Sponge: For cleaning work surfaces. You should have several of these.

Spring dividers: For measuring operations. See figure D, page 108.

Steel ruler: For accurate cutting. Used as a guide for mat knife.

Try-square: Used in cutting to ensure that all corners are cut precisely at an angle of 90 degrees. An essential.

Note: Additional tools will be individually specified as required in each project, such as a small piece of metal needed for protection while cutting.

A useful glossary

The following are the most frequently used bookbinder's terms:

Backing: Process of hammering the spine edge of the book's sections so that shoulders are formed, to which the cover boards may then be fitted. Shown in figure G, page 110.

Binder's board: Hard, dense, machine-made board, made from better grades of waste paper. Large, flat sheets of binder's board are cut down to the height and width of the book and are then covered with leather or cloth, to form the book's cover.

Case binding: Technique of making the cover of a book separately from the rest of the book and then attaching it.

Collating: Placing the book's sections or pages in consecutive order.

Cords: Pieces of linen or hemp twine on to which the sections of a book are sewn on a sewing frame. See figure F, page 109.

End papers: The folded sheets placed at the very front and back of a book. One half of each sheet is glued to the cover board.

Fore edge: The front edge of a book, opposite the spine edge.

Grain: In paper, the direction along which the fibres lie. The grain of the pages of a book must run from the head to the tail. To determine the direction of the grain, see photograph 2, page 106.

Head: The top edge of a book. The top of the pages of a book.

Headband: A piece of embroidery, either handmade or machine made, that is glued or stitched to the book at the very top of the spine.

Head cap: Portion of leather cover where the leather turns in at the head and tail of the spine. See photograph 29, page 113.

Kettle stitch: Chainlike stitch used to join the sections of a book just below the top and bottom of each section. See figure F, page 109.

Mull: Loosely woven cloth used to reinforce the book's spine.

Rounding: Shaping of the spine by hammering and by hand to force the spine into a more convex shape. See photograph 15, page 110.

Spine: The back or folded edge of the sections of a book, which are joined together by the sewing threads or cords.

Tail: The bottom edge of a book. The bottom of the pages.

Tipping in: Fastening one leaf of a book to another with a thin band of glue along one edge. See photographs 3 and 4, page 106.

Tooling: Decorating leather with heated finishing tools, using hand pressure and gold-foil application. Blind tooling refers to tooling that does not make use of coloured foils, but relies only on the heated tools to create the design. The tools darken the dampened leather when they come into direct contact with it.

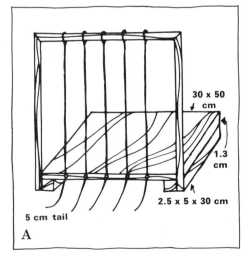

30 x 50 cm

1.3 cm

2.5 x 5 x 30 cm

5 cm tail

A

Figure A: A homemade sewing frame. This can be easily constructed out of wood, using a 30 by 50 cm piece of 1.3 cm plywood, two of 30 by 2.5 by 5 cm, and a few pieces of scrap moulding. Binder's cord is tied in a loop around the top crossbar, in the proper position, (see p. 109), and attached at the bottom by looping around a nail or thumb-tack. Tension on the cord can be adjusted by tying the loop with a tautline hitch or double half hitch. Make sure to sand the top edge of the crossbar round, so that the edge of the wood doesn't cut the cord.

Graphic Arts
Blue-Jean Cover

This first venture into bookbinding is for those who not only share a love
for unique-looking books, but have an interest in recycling cloth and a taste
for the whimsical. Search for a pair of old jeans you never wear any more.
Then find a book that has an uninteresting cloth cover. It is important that
the binding is still intact and the pages are in relatively good shape.
Commercially produced books have cloth-covered cases, glued to the already
bound text pages. Such cases come off rather easily.

Removing the old case

Place the book on a table, and open the front cover. The top sheet of paper,
the end paper, is a folded sheet; one half of it is pasted on to the board of
the cover, and the spine edge is tipped in with glue at the spine. Flip over
the end paper, so that you reveal the first right-hand page of your book.
Grasp the upper left edge of the end paper, and gently tug outwards until it
separates from the spine at the very top. Use the scalpel to cut through
the fabric mull, as shown in figure B. Work slowly. Repeat at the back of
the book. Peel or scrape off any excess glue or paper that is easily removed.

This is case binding with a flair for the original. An old pair of blue jeans is
transformed into new covering for a reference work, cookery book, textbook, or diary.
The pockets provide places to tuck pencils, pens, or note pads.

B

Figure B: Removing the old case. Flip
over front end paper; gently pull outwards
and away from spine. Cut down from top
through coarsely woven fabric mull until
cover falls away. Repeat at back of book.

Making new end papers

Select strong paper, and following the directions with photograph 2, find the direction of the grain. Now, bearing in mind that each sheet must have the grain running from the top to the bottom of the book, measure and cut two pieces exactly the height of the book and twice its width. Cut very carefully with a knife and try-square.

Bend one sheet in half by matching the corners of the two short ends. Holding this edge in place, use your other hand to place the bone folder at the side to be creased, and moving the folder away from you, press firmly across the fold. Repeat with second sheet. If cutting was exact, you now have two folded end papers of equal size, equal to the page size.

Tipping in the end papers

Place an end paper at the front of the book, lining up the folded edge with the spine and the three other edges with the page edges. With the folder, press along the small groove to the right of spine edge. Apply glue evenly, and tip in end paper, as in photographs 3 and 4. Repeat with back end paper. Let dry. Place book, spine up, between two boards in a press or vice.

Pasting on the mull

A piece of mull, 5 cm wider and 2.5 cm shorter than the spine, should now be applied. Follow directions for photographs 5 and 6.

2: Test to determine grain of the paper. Cut a small, rectangular piece from one edge, and moisten one side. Paper will curl up at a right angle to the grain.

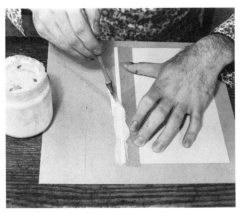

3: Press end paper into groove to crease it to fit into book. Apply a 6 mm band of glue to underside along spine edge. Mask with cardboard while applying glue.

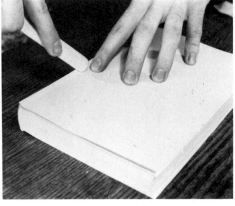

4: Lower end paper, glued side down, on to the book, lining up top, bottom, and spine edge. With bone folder, press firmly into the groove. Repeat for back end paper.

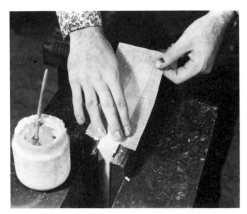

5: Apply glue to the spine, and centre the mull on the spine, leaving 1.3 cm of spine exposed at top and bottom. Apply glue evenly over the pasted-down mull.

6: Cut and apply glue to a piece of paper the size of the spine. While glue on mull is wet, place paper at top edge of spine, and guide in place down spine. Let dry.

7: Section of jeans, shown right side up. Waistband is trimmed off, as are heavy front and back seams, and at least 2 cm of fabric extends above pocket tops.

8: Place boards and spine piece on wrong side of cloth. Be sure to leave space of 6 mm between boards and spine piece. Line up pockets on boards. Trace outline.

9: After trimming and gluing (see text), turn right side up. With bone folder, rub firmly on to boards and spine piece, while pressing out any creases.

Making the new case

Cut the jeans apart so you have a flat piece of denim with two pockets, as shown in photograph 7. Now select a piece of binder's board of a thickness equal to the depth of the groove on each side of the spine. Measure and cut two pieces, each 6 mm longer than the height of the book and as wide as the total width from the groove to the fore edge. Make certain that all corners are square and that the corners of the two pieces line up exactly. Next, make the spine piece: Measure a piece of strong paper the height of the boards and the width of the spine. Cut carefully with a mat knife.

With the wrong side up, flatten the cloth on a table. Following the directions for photograph 8, place the boards and spine piece on the cloth. Once you have these three pieces correctly positioned and have a border at least 2 cm all around, trace the outline on the cloth. Remove the three pieces, and cut a rectangle, cutting 2 cm outside outline.

Using a large brush, apply glue evenly from centre of the cloth outwards, covering the entire area. One at a time, place the boards and spine piece within the tracing lines. Turn the whole thing over, and burnish firmly, as shown in photograph 9, flattening any creases. Next, trim the corners, and paste the edges to the boards, as outlined for figure C. Burnish on both sides with bone folder. Let case dry.

Position the book within the case, with 3 mm of the case protruding at the top, bottom, and fore edge and the spine lining up with the spine piece. Glue mull to the top end paper, as in photograph 10, and apply glue over the end paper's entire surface. Gently close the cover on to the end paper. Repeat for the back of the book. Place the book between two boards, as shown in photograph 11, and clamp in a vice until glue has dried. Remove the book, and rejoice! You are now a case binder.

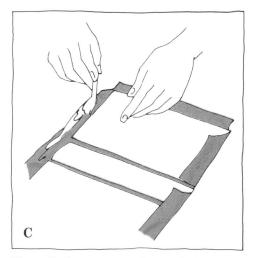

Figure C: Cut corners as shown—in at 45 degrees, out at 90 degrees. Apply glue to top and bottom edges, and turn down. Repeat for sides. Don't pull too tightly or boards will have a tendency to warp.

10: Insert waste sheet under the top end paper, and glue the mull to it. Apply glue outwards from centre until the entire surface of end paper is covered.

11: Two boards are placed up to the edge of the freshly cased book, so that the spine extends. Now clamp boards and book in a vice until the glue is dry.

Graphic Arts
Leather-Bound Diary

This diary-making project (see photograph on page 103) incorporates the full repertoire of the hand binder. The book pages are folded, lined up, and sewed on to cords. The cords are laced on to cover boards, and the boards covered with leather. A panel of contrasting leather is inlaid on the cover, and gold foil is tooled overall. The process can take an expert up to eight hours. It would be wise to set aside three full days for this project, or plan to devote part of each day to it for a week or more.

Selecting leather and paper

No book is as sensuous as a leather-bound one. Pleasing to the touch, it improves with care. Supple, acid-free goat or calfskin is the best to use, as this will retard decay. Obtain the leather at a leather shop.

It is of great importance to select the proper paper for your book pages, one that is durable and good-looking. The best paper is handmade. Though expensive, it will last longer than machine-made paper. A good alternative is 100 per cent rag paper. A sheet of paper 21.5 by 28 cm, when folded in half, yields a page size 14 cm wide by 21.5 cm high. Order a size that appeals to your eye when the paper is folded.

Making the sections of the book

Take three sheets of paper and line up the edges. Hold the three together; bend in half, and press down with the folder to crease. You have now made one section. Continue making sections until the book measures 2.5 cm thick when all sections are pressed tightly together into a stack. Line up sections, and place between boards, with folded edges up.

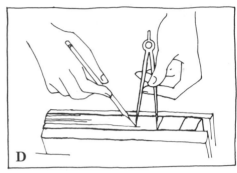

Figure D: With folded side of sections up, use spring dividers to position five equally spaced lines. Start 1.3 cm from one end, and space lines so space between fifth line and the opposite end is the same as space between the lines. The line with the extra 1.3 cm space will be the bottom of your book, and the extra space here will aid in proper stacking on the sewing frame. Following the lines with a hacksaw blade, lightly cut slots across the spine just deep enough to allow for the width of a piece of binder's cord.

This interior view of the handbound leather-covered diary shows coloured and polished top edge, handsewn headband in two colours, and marble-patterned end paper detail.

Preparation for sewing

Clamp the sections between the boards in a press or vice. Use spring dividers and a pencil, follow the instructions for figure D, opposite. After you have sawn five grooves, draw a line at each end, halfway between the groove and the very edge. Saw lightly. These will be for the kettle stitch.

You will need a sewing frame. Construct one, referring to figure A, page 104 which gives dimensions and instructions.

Place the sections of the book on the frame with the folded edges facing the cords. Move the cords so they line up exactly with the grooves. When the cords are correctly placed, tie them down. Remove all except the bottom section, and fit the cords snugly into its grooves.

Sewing the sections together

Sit at the frame, with the cords and grooved edge of the section facing you. Cut a comfortable length of thread, and run it across beeswax three or four times, to prevent the thread's kinking or cutting the paper. Put one end of the thread through the eye of the needle. Then stick the point of the needle through the same end of thread. This will lock the thread on to the needle. Open the section to its middle, as shown in photograph 12. Insert the needle at the kettle-stitch groove on the left end, and push needle through to the inside of the section. Leave a tail of two inches of thread where you inserted the needle. You will pick this up later.

Now, from the inside of the section, insert the needle so that it comes out to the right of the first cord. Reinsert the needle to the left of the cord, and pull needle back to the inside of the section. Sew around the other four cords in the same manner. When pulling thread, pull parallel to the spine (see figure E for all angles). The thread is being drawn along the inside fold of the section, coming outside only to encircle each cord. Encircle all five cords; push needle from the inside to the outside so it emerges at right-hand kettle-stitch groove. Press top of section between cords with the bone folder to make sure it is flat and even.

Place the next section on the sewing frame. Insert the needle at the right-hand kettle-stitch groove of the second section. Pull through to inside of section, and working back towards the left side, encircle cords in the opposite direction. Come out at kettle-stitch groove on left side. Knot loose tail to thread where it emerges from second-section left-side kettle-stitch groove. Press down between cords with your bone folder, and now insert needle at kettle-stitch groove of third section. Sew across. At the right kettle-stitch groove of third section, make kettle stitch, as shown in figure F. Press down with folder. Insert needle in fourth section.

12: Sit comfortably at sewing frame, with folded side of sections towards you. Open first section to centre fold; then sew.

Figure F: Making the kettle stitch. At right kettle-stitch line of third section and from then on, bring needle from right to left through the stitch just below; then put the needle through the loop formed as you pull the thread. Now insert needle into kettle-stitch mark of next section above. This will lock sections at the top and bottom of the spine. Drawing at left shows kettle stitch made at left kettle-stitch line; drawing at right, stitched sections.

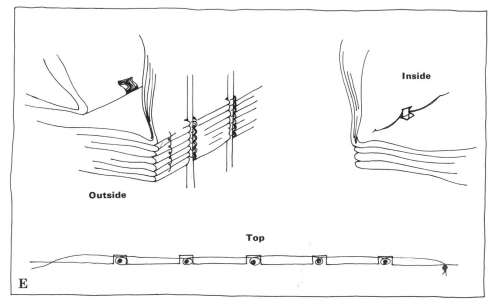

Inside

Outside

Top

E

Figure E: Sections shown on sewing frame from three angles: inside, outside, top.

Continue making kettle-stitches at the end of each new section and pressing section between cords with bone folder. If you start to run out of thread, neatly knot on another strand so the knot falls between cords. When the last section has been sewn on, end with two kettle-stitches made into the same stitch. Cut thread. All sewing is now done. Remove book from sewing frame, as shown in photograph 13. Tip in a sheet of waste paper at the front and back. Place sewn sections between boards in press or vice.

Rounding and backing the book
To round, apply glue over the spine, as shown in photograph 14. Remove from the press, and work with your hand and a hammer, as in photograph 15. Work on both sides, gently drawing outer sections towards you. Now replace book in the press, spine up, at a distance from the edges of the boards equal to the thickness of the cover boards, as in photograph 16.

To back, follow directions for figure G. Work slowly to achieve well-formed

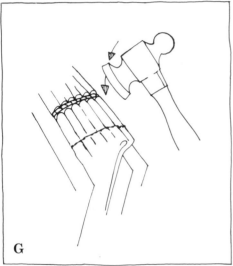

G

Figure G: Backing. Again apply glue down the spine. Now, with glancing blows from the spine outwards, shape the spine. Hold hammer close to its head. As you work, make sure that, though being formed, all sections remain parallel. If the glue starts to dry, brush on more. Continue working carefully until shoulders form a right angle to the back. This may take up to half an hour. Be patient.

13: When sewing is completed, detach the cords 5 cm below the book. Then cut the cords 5 cm above the top of the book. Do not cut the top cords first.

14: Clamp the book, spine up, between backing boards in press or vice. Keep cords on shoulders of boards as you apply glue over the spine with a brush.

15: Rounding. Push in with thumb at the fore edge while gently hammering side of spine. Turn book over, and repeat this.

16: Preparing for backing. Space between top of backing boards and backbone must equal the thickness of the cover board.

shoulders. You are now making what will be final shape of the book spine.

With book still in the press, cut off both ends of the second and fourth cords. Unravel the remaining three cords, as shown in photograph 17.

The next step—applying paint and beeswax to the top edge—can succeed only if the top edge of your book is level and smooth. The professional uses a hand plough with a very sharp blade to trim the page tops to the same height. You can do this by clamping the book tightly to a table. Mark a line 3 mm from the top of the first page. With a steel ruler and a very sharp knife, cut across the line, sheet by sheet, until the entire top of

17: Carefully cut off second and fourth cords. With your fingers and a needle, remove glue from the remaining three cords, while unravelling the strands.

18: Trim top edge, and paint lightly with watercolour. Then rub beeswax firmly over entire top edge. With folder, burnish in beeswax to remove excess and to polish.

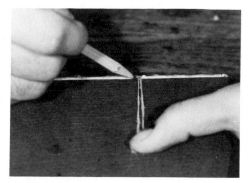

19: Line up cover board with spine edge of book until it lies in shoulder groove. Bring each cord across cover board, and mark its position carefully on the board.

20: With scalpel, make shallow, V-shape notch wherever you have marked for the cords. Do not cut through the board. Work on one side only of each board.

21: Cords are laced through the boards from the outside (notched part) of the board to the inside. Apply glue in each hole and hammer flat, so hole closes.

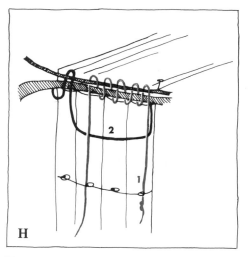

Figure H: Cut two pieces of binder's cord, 1.3 cm longer than the width of spine. Coat each evenly with glue. Let dry. Put a pin through both cords at one end, and stick at end of book through waste sheet. Choose two colours of silk buttonhole thread. Cut a 30 cm piece of one, a 46-cm piece of the other. Knot together at one end. Thread a needle on loose end of 46-cm piece (1). Push needle through spine from the inside of centre of first section, just below the kettle stitches. Bring short thread (2) over top of spine and under the bottom cord next to pin. With threaded piece, make figure-of-eight stitches around the cords as shown. Cross over with short thread, and repeat stitch, starting under the bottom cord. Continue, alternating colours. At the next to last stitch of every other band of the colour with the needle, go under bottom cord and inside centre of adjacent section, out through spine below kettle stitch as in (1), and up under bottom cord again. This will tie down headband. Continue stitch. At the end, tie down twice. Cut threads, leaving 1.3 cm, and glue to spine. Glue over back of headband. Cut off cords where threads end. Remove pin. Repeat at tail if desired.

the book is evenly cut. Now clamp the book, top edge up, very tightly in the press. Apply watercolour paint over the surface of the top edge. When dry, polish as shown in photograph 18.

Making headbands

Headbands protect the head cap and give the book a finished look. Study figure H, and if you think the procedure too difficult, skip this section. If you wish to make headbands, get two pieces of cord, one thicker than the other, spools of contrasting-colour silk thread, a needle, and a straight pin. Use the pin to spear the two cords, thin over thick for small stitches on top row, to the very top of the book at the far right corner of the first section. Carefully follow the directions for figure H. Repeat procedure at the tail if you wish.

Making cover boards and lacing cords to cover

Cut binder's board into two pieces, each 3 mm wider than the book from the shoulder to the fore edge and 6 mm longer than the height of the spine. One at a time, line up the boards with the book at the spine groove, with 3 mm of the boards protruding at head and tail. Mark the spine edge for the position of the cords, as shown in photograph 19.

Make notches, as in photograph 20. With an awl, pierce the board at the point of every V. Using photograph 21, lace on the boards, hammering the holes closed with glue as you go. The side you hammer is not the side with the notches; they are on outside of board. Hammer the inside of the board, where only the holes are visible.

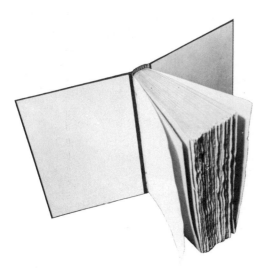

22: Now line inside of boards. Cut paper 3 mm smaller than board, and stick down with flour paste (recipe, opposite page), smoothing with bone folder.

Preparing for covering

There are several things to be done before you apply the leather cover.

Line the inside of the boards with paper, as shown in photograph 22. This will counteract warping of the boards when the damp leather is pasted on to the boards' front. This paper acts as a stabilizer.

Cut away slivers of board at top and bottom of the spine edge, as shown in photograph 23. This will enable the covers to open and close easily, even though there will be a double thickness of leather at these places, where you will turn down the leather on the inside of the boards.

23: Put metal square under spine edge. Cut sliver 2 mm wide, 1.3 cm long.

24: Place strong paper over the length of the spine. Make sure the grain of the paper is running the length of the spine. Holding paper over the spine as shown, mark the width of the spine on it.

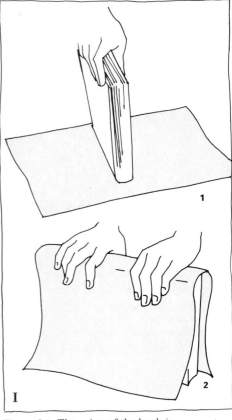

Figure I-1: The spine of the book is carefully lowered into place on the pared leather. Now leather is brought up on to the boards, one side at a time.
Figure I-2: Flip book over on table.

25: Place the ruler at spine-width mark. Fold the paper over towards ruler, and crease with bone folder. Fold over once more. Draw a line where this ends.

26: Pare a semicircle from the leather · beneath head and tail of spine. Gently thin down to a feathered edge, so leather will be easy to tuck under hollow back.

27: Hold book up while letting covers fall open. Work leather under the hollow back, leaving out width of headband, to make head cap. Smooth down edge, and flatten with the bone folder, so the leather is pressed down. Repeat at tail.

28: Turn leather over at fore edge. With bone folder, bring corner to a 45-degree angle. Cut off corner leather 6 mm above book. Pick up fore edge, and fold the piece of leather from top edge under it. Fold fore edge back down.

29: A slip loop is tied around the book from the head to the tail of the spine. Thread should be fitted tightly into the grooves to the side of the spine, which you cut in photograph 23. Using pointed bone folder, pull out leather between cord and headband on both sides. With flat bone folder, beat down the top of the leather until it is of a pleasing shape. Repeat this at the tail edge.

Now make the hollow back. Follow directions for photographs 24 and 25. After you have folded the paper twice, draw a line where folded page ends. Open the paper. Cut along line. Now apply glue to the area adjacent to your cutting line. Refold paper as before, so that it adheres to the glued area, forming a tube. Cut to length of spine, adding a bit extra for the height of headbands. One side of this tube is a single thickness of paper, and the other side is a double thickness. The single side is now glued on to the spine and smoothed out.

You may now cut the leather. Place the leather, wrong side up, on a table. Lay your closed book on top of the leather. Mark around the edges carefully, and mark the position of the corners of the board near the spine. Without shifting the book's position on the leather, roll it over on to the other cover, and mark in the same way. Put the book aside. Draw a line 2 cm from line you have marked, all around. Cut with shears along this outer line.

With either a paring or skiving knife, slightly pare down the wrong side of the leather over the original line you drew around the book, so that when the leather here is turned over the edges of the boards, it will lie smoothly. Then pare a semicircle, outside the original line, on the section of the leather that will be folded under the spine, around the hollow back, at the top and the bottom, as illustrated in photograph 26.

Next, prepare some wheat-flour paste: Mix unbleached flour with cold water until it is the consistency of thick cream. Cook over medium heat, stirring constantly, until the mixture is transformed into paste. Let cool. This paste is also used on paper covering boards (photograph 22).

Applying the leather cover
Dampen right side of the leather so that it is quite wet. Coat wrong side of the leather thinly with paste. Work from the centre outwards. Wait five minutes. Then apply a thin second coat of paste over the first one.

Very carefully lower the spine of the book on to the centre of the leather, as in figure I-1. Gently lift one side of the leather up and on to the cover board. Holding this side in place, gently lift the other side on to the other board. Turn the book over, as in figure I-2. Smooth the leather over the spine and sides with your fingers, being careful not to stretch the damp leather or make any marks in it.

Turn the book over, so that the covers are open, and follow directions for photograph 27. Work slowly, using the bone folder. Next, follow the instructions for photograph 28. Repeat this process on all the edges.

Make a slip loop of linen thread, and tie it around the spine, from head to tail of the book, as shown from top in photograph 29. The knot you make

should fall between the boards at the bottom edge, so it will not damage the surface of the leather. Wet leather marks easily, so beware of long fingernails and table edges. Now form the head cap, as shown in photograph 29, page 113. A lump exists at the inside edge of the board, near the head cap. Smooth this down by sliding in the flat bone folder and pressing out, without opening the book. Do not open book now. Smooth spine again with fingers; make sure leather has completely adhered.

Place a piece of cardboard between the book and the cover up to the string. Then place a clean sheet of paper, a wooden board, and a brick on the book. Let them remain overnight, while leather dries.

Remove the book from under board and brick. Take out cardboard. Open the front cover. With spring dividers, locate a point inside the cover, equidistant from the fore-edge and bottom edge. Line up steel ruler so that it touches the very tip of the bottom corner and this point, in a diagonal path. Cut leather along this line with scalpel. Lift off waste. Now lift fore-edge, and remove the piece beneath it, as in photograph 30. Reapply paste, and press down with bone folder. The corner is now mitred. Repeat this procedure for the three remaining corners of the book; work slowly.

To trim the edge, mark around the edges at a distance equal to the narrowest part of the turn in. Cut squarely on this line, so all turn ins are now even. Cut a piece of thin cardboard to fit exactly within the turn

▲ Applying gold-foil tooling to the leather cover. Foil is dull side down on cover. Tool has been heated to the correct temperature and is hand pressed through the foil on to the cover leather.

▼ A pointed tool is used to clean away excess gold. An awl or divider point can be used for this. A soft rubber will remove any remaining specks of gold.

30: Mitring the corners of the turn in. Work slowly, with scalpel, to remove excess leather from under the fore edge. Reapply paste, and set back in place.

31: Measuring before trimming end paper. Make sure that the width of the turn in showing under the pasted-down end paper is uniform all around inside of cover.

in, filling in the area. Glue cardboard into position. Remove waste sheets.

Now fold a piece of marbled paper so the pattern is inside and the size is that of your pages. Tip in, but do not paste down on to board. First, trim the part of end paper to be pasted down, so that, when pasted, it will extend 3 mm beyond the edge of the cardboard, over the leather. Placing a waste sheet underneath, apply paste to entire end paper. Then add glue to the 6 mm that will cover the joint. Wait 15 seconds. Work this into joint with fingers and folder.

Now paste down the rest of end paper. With folder, work out creases through waste paper. Keep cover open for 10 minutes, so paste can adhere completely. Then work on the back end paper.

To make contrasting leather insert, cut a shape from the piece of leather, and paste it on to the cover of the book. Cut around edge of insert with a scalpel. Peel up this piece and the piece beneath it, and separate them. Then paste the insert in place.

To tool with gold foil, place foil dull side down where you want gold to appear. Heat a metal tool over an open flame until, when tested, it hisses on a wet rag. Press the tool through the foil on to the leather.

Tools for imprinting initials range from as low as £1 for some single initials to £30 or more for complete sets, which are available in varying patterns from craft and leather shops.

BOOK-CARE CRAFTNOTES

Repairing Torn Pages

First of all, never use cellophane tape to repair any portion of a book. That much said, repairing torn pages is not as impossible a feat as you may think. The secret of well-mended tears is called Japanese tissue. A more transparent variety is called Japanese silk tissue. Both kinds are well worth owning. To mend a torn sheet, simply tear a strip of Japanese tissue, about 1.3 cm wide, that follows the direction of the tear in the page. Get out your homemade wheat-flour paste (see page 113), and apply a thin layer to the tissue. Paste tissue over the tear, holding sides of tear close together. Burnish with bone folder through a piece of paper. Let dry, and the repair is completed.

Taking a Book Apart

Unless the book is very old, in which case you should take it to an expert, remove its cover following directions given on page 105. If you want to take the sections apart, you must remove the sewing threads at the centre of each section. Put book, spine up, in a vice. Scrape off glue with a knife. If glue still adheres, apply a coat of flour paste, and let it stand five minutes. Scrape. If this doesn't work, apply toluene very carefully to soften the glue. Open the book to the centre of first section. With a scalpel, cut exposed threads. Gently lift out the section. Continue this process with each section. With a little patience and a sharp scalpel, you will soon have the sections of your book separated and ready for resewing or repairing or whatever you wish to do.

Deacidifying and Oiling Leather

Sulphur dioxide is a major air pollutant. If leather is allowed to dry out, it will be attacked by this gas, which, in the presence of oxygen and water vapour, will turn into sulphuric acid. The acid will destroy the cellular structure of leather, turning it eventually into dust. Regular deacidification and oiling, every two to three years, will prevent this. To deacidify leather, a seven-per cent solution of potassium lactate is used. Apply this evenly, with a soft cloth, over the entire surface of the leather. Then oil the leather with a mixture of half lanolin and half neat's-foot oil. This mixture should be rubbed in gently with your hand, using a circular motion.
Make sure all areas of the leather surfaces are well-coated with the mixture. Then let the book stand for a day or two while oil soaks into the leather. Finally, use soft cloth to buff and polish all leather surfaces.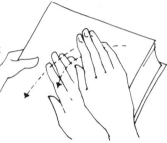

Cleaning Cloth Covers

Use a bookbinder's dry-cleaning agent, and follow the directions on the bottle label.

Dry-Cleaning Soiled Pages

Grind up several gum rubbers, and rub the small particles over the soiled page. They will pick up any surface dirt. Rubber crumbs can be saved and re-used.

If pages are still soiled, they will need to be washed or bleached. Do not attempt to do this yourself. Consult an expert and, if possible, have him do it.

Deacidifying Paper

If the book pages turn yellow or brittle, the cause is acid in the paper. This is a result of production methods which use wood pulp that deteriorates quickly, forming acid. A product used to deacidify the paper is a solution of magnesium methoxide. It comes in a spray bottle and should be carefully sprayed, as directed on the label, on all pages of a yellowing book. The paper will not look any different after you have deacidified it but the treatment will slow the process of deterioration.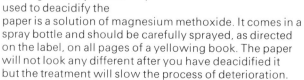

By now you can probably make the routine repairs your books require. For books on solving more complex repair problems, consult your local library.

BOTTLE CUTTING
Turn Old into New

By Walter Ian Fischman

There was a time when all household bottles, having served their original purposes, were piled into one of three heaps—the collectable, the returnable, and the disposable. What was once returnable or disposable can now be made re-usable and sometimes even converted into attractive collectables when modified by modern methods of bottle cutting. Though you will not save the environment single-handedly, bottle cutting is in the spirit of conservation because it reclaims what would otherwise be wasted.

Take a walk through your supermarket and note the array of products in glass containers. Though you will see many forms and sizes, watch for those that are cylindrically shaped. They are the easiest to cut. Cutting square and irregular shapes calls for a great deal of skill, and even then the rate of failure is quite high.

The secret, if there is one, of producing a good-looking object lies not in the actual cutting technique—in most cases that is simple enough. More important to the end result is the development of a simple design based on the shape of the bottle. Study the bottle, looking for lines that please you. Occasionally you may want the effect given by embossing, lettering, or labels, but the general rule is to choose a design that will yield a useful object without too much novelty.

Each bottle has the potential of becoming at least one other object. For example, a beer bottle makes a good-looking tumbler if you cut off the neck and sand the edge smooth. Inexpensive bottles, of course, will not yield Waterford crystal, but they will make handsome and useful objects if you give some thought to form and design and execute the actual cutting with care and precision.

Glass and Plastics
Basics of Cutting

Bottle cutting is, basically, nothing more than glass cutting—or causing glass to break where you want it to break. There are two methods. One takes advantage of the fact that a three-cornered file will scratch a line in glass. The other utilizes the standard glass-cutter principle: roll a sharp-edge wheel across glass, and it will cause minute particles of the glass to chip away, leaving a definite and deep scratch. In both cases, the glass tends to break, under stress, along the scratch—although sometimes it proves stubborn and breaks in every direction.

The most common type of bottle cutter—the kind that rests in the mouth of the bottle and features a metal arm that breaks the glass by tapping the score from the inside—is effective to a certain extent. However, tapping from the inside of the bottle makes possible the hazard of flying particles of glass. Also, the cuts produced by this device tend to be less clean than those obtained by other methods.

If you decide to try the three-cornered-file method, you will have to construct the simple jig shown in figure B on page 118. It guides the bottle, producing a perfect scratch line. To make it, you need a piece of 2.5-by-15 cm

A

Figure A: Cut a large pickle jar just below the shoulder to make canister, or midway to make planter. A 100 g baby-food jar cut below the shoulder makes a good spice jar. Sand the edges smooth, and close with 5 cm-thick cork. For clarity in this drawing and drawings that follow, bottles are represented both flat and three-dimensionally.

Transparent kitchen containers made from baby-food and pickle jars. A spice jar, canister, or planter can be made with only one cut with a bottle cutter.

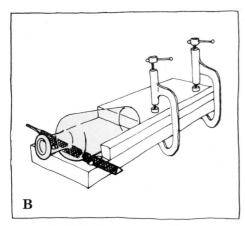

Figure B: Make the jig you need for extreme accuracy in bottle cutting by nailing the 2.5 by 2.5 (with glue) along the edge of the 2.5 by 15 cm. Position the three-cornered file at exactly right angles across the end, and fasten it with the flathead screws. The short length of 2.5 by 10 cm, clamped in place, forms the stop against which the bottom of the bottle rides, while the side of the bottle rides the fence formed by the 2.5 by 2.5.

1: After filing a groove around the bottle with the jig, left, tie a piece of string tightly in the groove. Cut off the ends. Be sure the string is tight.

2: Saturate the string with lighter fuel; then ignite it with a match. This subjects the bottle to intense heat along the score mark, where it is weakest.

3: When the flame dies, dunk the bottle in a pail of cold water. The sudden change in temperature causes the glass to fracture along the score line.

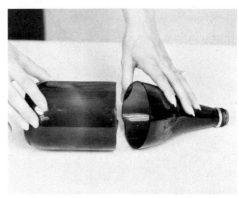

4: Nine times out of ten, the bottle sections will fall apart. If they don't, pull them gently, or tap lightly with the handle of a screwdriver or knife.

timber about 45 cm long, a piece of 2.5-by-10 about 15 cm long, a 38-cm-long piece of 2.5-cm square moulding, two C clamps, a three-cornered file, and four 2.5-cm No. 10 flathead screws. To construct the jig, follow directions for figure B. To use it, position the piece of 2.5-by-10, according to the size of the bottle and the location of the cut. Holding the bottle against it and the 2.5-cm moulding, rotate the bottle once on the file.

The basic steps for making clean breaks in bottle cutting are illustrated above: this method involves heating the glass, then cooling it suddenly. This process is used after a bottle is scored with the homemade jig described in the text above and on the preceding page.

You may also be able to obtain a bottle-cutter from stores or craft shops, or from mail order houses that advertise in craft and hobby magazines. No matter which method you use, here are some helpful and useful suggestions:

Make a few practice cuts on some bottles you don't care about, until you have mastered a technique that works every time.

Observe sensible safety rules: Be careful handling fresh-cut, razor-sharp edges; wear goggles while cutting; don't work on a bottle with its cap on—it might explode if you are using the heat-cold method.

Don't try to cut a dirty bottle or one with the label on it; the paper and glue would prevent the glass cutter or file from scoring effectively.

Be sure to use the kind of sandpaper that is coated with aluminium oxide—

not standard flint paper. (Aluminium-oxide paper is sometimes called production paper.) For the smooth edges necessary for drinking glasses, sand with a special paper called wet and dry, and use it wet to keep down glass dust, which can be hazardous.

Whenever you work on a project that requires gluing and must withstand heat, such as the trivet shown on page 120, use a special adhesive called epoxy cement, sold at hardware shops. It comes in two tubes, containing resin and hardener, which must be mixed. Some varieties dry in five minutes. If the object will not be subjected to heat, silicone adhesives will do.

Bottles come in such a variety of shapes, colours and sizes that they make a fascinating collection; look out for old or unusual ones.

Make a "stained-glass" window out of an ordinary window by gluing bottle bottoms, in various colours, to the windowpane. No sanding required. Tape each round in place until glue is dry. Paint the window between the rounds (see text, page 121).

Figure C: To make window rounds in colour photograph above, cut assorted bottles of same diameter 4 cm from bottom.

This novel serving trivet was made from seven 2.5 cm-wide glass rings. Cut them from a single wine bottle, beginning at the top of the bottle and working down.

These hanging lamps cast interesting shadows and highlights due to the irregularities in the glass of the wine bottles and water jugs from which they were made. Begin the project by cutting off the base of a 4.5 litre jug. Scoring the neck all the way around is impossible because the handle gets in the way, but score as far as possible, and proceed to the heating process. The diameter of the neck is so small and the glass so thick that the fracture will go across the unscored glass with repeated heating and rotating. An irregular cut is of little importance in this case. Tap the jug to complete the cut. Slip this outer shell over the uncut wine bottle until it rests on the wine bottle's shoulder. This is to determine where the wine bottle should be cut. Its bottom edge should be about 4 cm higher than the bottom edge of the cut jug. If you are making more than one lamp, score duplicate cuts before moving the footplate on your bottle cutter. Sand bottom edges of bottle and jug lightly. Thread electrical cord through both until they rest on an attached light-bulb socket.

No doubt your first bottle-cutting endeavours will be in the area of mugs and tumblers, but don't stop there. The hanging lamps and the trivet shown on this page are simple to make and take very little time. Both are worth the bother, in terms of the extra interest they will provide in your home. The bottles and jugs involved are standard and easy to find.

D

Figure D: To make outer shell of hanging lamp, cut a 4.5 litre jug at the bottom and at base of the neck. A wine bottle cut at the bottom forms the inner shell.

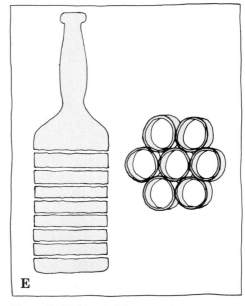

E

Figure E: Eight cuts 2.5 cm apart on a wine bottle produce the seven rings necessary for the trivet shown in the photograph above. Sand both cut edges; apply epoxy to the parts of the rings that touch each other, and hold together with clothes pegs until glue is dry.

Glass and Plastics
Decorating Bottles

After you have made a few cut-bottle objects and have mastered the cutting technique, you may wish to go a step farther by decorating their surfaces in various ways. You can paint coloured designs on the glass, or you can glue assorted decorative materials on the surface for a novel effect.

The vase in the colour photograph at the right and the bottle-covered window on page 119 were given a stained-glass appearance with transparent paint for glass and an ink marking pen. The special see-through paint, in a variety of colours, is available at most craft and hobby shops. It takes longer to dry than most paints, so be prepared to allow more time for projects that make use of it. Remember that such decorated surfaces can be cleaned with a soft, damp cloth only, since neither the paint nor the marker can withstand detergents or hot water.

The glasses in the colour photograph below were painted with opaque, lead-free enamel. The brown juice glass, formerly a plain beer bottle, was given a bold stripe. A wine bottle, cut at midpoint, was painted with flowers, to produce a party tumbler. To paint the flowers, make a central dot and then six or seven brush strokes outwards from that centre. Make as many flowers as you wish. Paint a stem with one long sweep from the bottom of the flower to the bottom of the glass. Brush strokes show when you paint with enamel on glass; but if you use them cleverly, they provide interesting and natural-looking designs.

As an example of one of the many effects you can achieve with glued-on decorations, look at the bud vase shown in the colour photograph on page 122. It is covered with 2.5-cm metal squares, applied shingle fashion. The squares were cut from a narrow Venetian-blind slat. You can do that, or cut them from a sheet of softer metal such as aluminium, available at many hardware shops. String, shells, stamps, or the original bottle labels are other possibilities for glue-ons. And don't forget to try other crafts, such as stencilling or decoupage, for decorating your cut bottles.

This vase is a soda-water bottle with its top cut off and its edge sanded. Its stained-glass design was achieved with transparent paint and an ink marking pen.

Bold stripes and delicate flowers adorn these tumblers made of cut bottles. You can make your own set of free party glasses like these in just a few hours.

▼ The bud vase was made from two pieces of a soda bottle and covered with metal squares. Epoxy glue holds top and bottom of cut bottle together (figure F). Then 2.5 cm metal squares were glued on shingle fashion. To cover the vase, begin at bottom and work around and up sides.

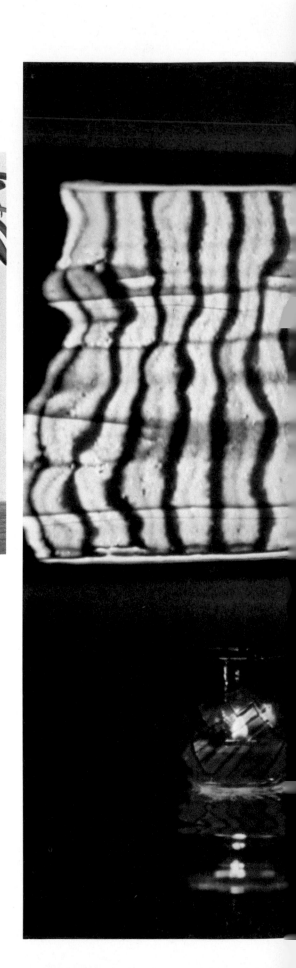

Figure F: Middle of soda-water bottle, above left, makes cylinder for hurricane lamp in large photograph. Top and bottom, glued together, form vase, above right.

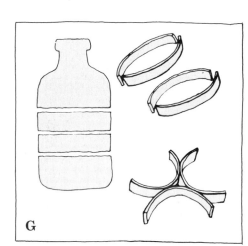

Figure G: The candleholder for the hurricane lamp was made from rings 2 cm wide cut from a beer bottle. Hold each ring with a cloth, and cut it into semicircles by scoring with a hand-held cutter and tapping apart.

▶Shimmering lights are created by candles held in cut-bottle objects and windows reflecting in shiny background. The three small votive candles burn inside containers made from 100 g baby-food jars, cut just below the shoulder. They were painted with a random pattern in red, maroon, and yellow transparent paint outlined with an indelible felt marker. The hurricane cylinder shielding the taper, centre, was the middle section of a soda-water bottle (figure F). The base holding the taper was made from rings cut from a beer bottle. With a hand-held cutter, the rings were scored so that they could be broken into two semicircles (figure G). Three of them were glued with epoxy glue. The candle is inserted in the central opening formed when the three semicircles were joined. The hurricane cylinder simply rests on this trivet-like candleholder. Once you become attuned to possibilities such as these, you will be making many other objects out of bottles.

BOTTLE GARDENS
Nature in Miniature

By James McNair and Bob Springman

Bottle gardens had their beginnings in 1829, when a scientist, Nathaniel Ward, placed a chrysalis in a closed glass jar with garden soil. When seeds and fern spores that were in the soil grew and flourished in the jar, he realized that plants can exist in a microcosm. This discovery led to his invention of glass cases that nurtured plants during long sea voyages.

Later in the 19th century, Dr. Ward's glass box became a display case, suitably ornamented for Victorian drawing rooms, where it housed delicate ferns, rare orchids, and other tropical plants.

Dr. Ward's concept is today's answer to gardening in areas where atmospheric pollution or dry air presents problems. In a sealed jar or in a bottle with a small opening, plants can create an ecologically balanced microcosm of nature. As an introduction to bottle gardening, try a variation on Ward's original experiment. In a clean, litre canning jar, not tinted, place a cup of moist soil from garden, wood or roadside. (Although we recommend purchased potting soil for bottle gardens, it will not work for this experiment, because it has been pasteurized.) Screw on the lid, and set the jar in bright light and where the temperature is comfortable for you. After a few days, the soil will show signs of plant growth.

Greenery and Growing Things
Water-Cooled Landscape

Select any of the plants we suggest here, or others known to thrive in high humidity. They should also be of small size and slow-growing.

To duplicate our garden, you will need a clear-glass carboy, about a half a litre each of clean, sharp sand (builder's, not from the seashore), pea gravel, charcoal chips, and purchased potting soil; plants shown in figure A, page 126, or chosen from the list on the left; and pieces of any green moss collected in the woods, or florist's sheet moss, sufficient to cover a 25-cm square. As finishing touches, you might add bits of weathered

Plants for Bottle Gardens

In addition to the plants shown in figures A and B, pages 126 and 127, select any of the small-growing plants listed below.

Acorus gramineus variegatus—Miniature Sweet Flag
Adiantum tenerum wrightii—A maidenhair fern
Bertolonia hirsuta—Jewel plant
Boea hygroscopica—Oriental streptocarpus
Calathea micans—Miniature maranta
Carex foliosissima var. albo-mediana— Miniature variegated sedge
Cissus striata—Miniature grape ivy
Cryptanthus bivittatus roseo-pictus— Dwarf rose-stripe star
Dionaea muscipula—Venus flytrap
Dracaena godseffiana 'Florida Beauty'
Episcia reptans—Scarlet African violet
Fittonia verschaffeltii—Mosaic plant
Gesneria cuneifolia—Fire cracker
Hedera helix—Miniature English ivy
Isoloma amabilis—Tree gloxinia
Maranta leuconeura kerchoveana—Prayer plant
Neanthe elegans—Dwarf palm
Philodendron sodiroi—Silver-leaf philodendron
Pilea muscosa—Artillery plant
Pteris ensiformis 'Victoriae'—Victoria table fern
Saintpaulia ionantha, miniature cultivars— African violet
Saxifraga stolonifera—Mother of Thousands
Terranema mexicanum—Mexican foxglove

1: Tools for bottle gardening are, from left, syringe for watering and cleaning leaves, poker for positioning elements, camel-hair brush, wooden tongs, mechanic's pick-up tool, and funnel.

2: The growing media essential for a successful bottle garden include, from left, pea-size stones or gravel, home-mixed or purchased potting soil, charcoal chips, and clean, sharp sand.

Set in bright light, but not direct sun, a clear glass water-cooler bottle nurtures a miniature landscape. Inset shows tiny *Sophronitis coccinea* orchids inside.

wood or pretty stones or sea shells small enough to slip through the bottle's 2.5-cm neck. For tools, we used those shown in photograph 1, page 124, plus a double thickness of newspaper coiled to extend the funnel, but you can get by with only the syringe, tongs, and a paper funnel.

When you have assembled all the materials, proceed as follows:

☐ Clean and polish inside of bottle, using tongs, paper towel, and, if the bottle is very soiled, window-cleaning spray. Let dry.

☐ Using funnel with paper extender shown in photograph 4, add 2.5-cm layers of sand, charcoal chips, and, finally, potting soil.

☐ Set bottle on sheet of paper; trace around it with a pencil. Assemble your small potted plants inside the circle in a pleasing arrangement.

☐ Beginning with the larger, sturdier plants and finishing with the more delicate miniatures, remove one plant at a time from its pot. Shake or wash away in tepid water most of the soil clinging to the root system. Slip small plants through the bottle neck. It may be easier to wind large plants in a cone of paper, as shown in photograph 7 and figure C, page 128.

3: Holding paper towel with wooden tongs polish inside of bottle. Window-cleaning spray helps remove stains. Let the bottle dry completely before garden is planted.

4: Use a cylinder of paper to extend the funnel when you add dusty materials, such as charcoal chips and potting soil. This helps keep inside of glass clean.

5: To remove a plant from its pot, place one hand across the soil surface; turn pot nearly upside down, and give it a sharp whack. The root ball will come free.

6: Rinse away most of the soil from root system before putting plant in bottle. Work carefully, so as not to break or bruise tender roots, leaves, and stems.

Figure A: Bottle garden includes eight different plants, chosen for contrast in leaf texture and colour, and for seasonal bloom. They are (1) *Sophronitis coccinea* (a small orchid), (2) 'Persian Brocade' begonia (fibrous rooted), (3) *Selaginella delicatula* (a moss fern), (4) *Sinningia pusilla* (miniature Gloxinia), (5) *Asplenium nidus* (Bird's-nest fern), (6) *Oxalis oregana*, (7) *Asplenium cristatum* (a spleenwort fern), and (8) *Selaginella serpens* (one of several plants referred to as moss fern; the selaginellas are allied botanically with ferns, but they are neither true ferns nor true mosses). Garden is pictured in colour on page 125.

A

B

Figure B: Laboratory bottle is a study in geology with its clearly defined layers of pea gravel, charcoal, sand, soil. Plants: (1) *Begonia dregei var. macbethii* (miniature maple-leaf begonia), (2) *Selaginella emmeliana* (moss fern), (3) *Ficus pumila var. minima* (miniature creeping fig), (4) *Pedilanthus tithymaloides cucullata* (Bird Cactus), (5) *Begonia x richmondensis* in pot, (6) *Selaginella plumosa* (cushion moss), and (7) *Helxine soleirolii 'Aurea'* (Golden Baby Tears).

◄ A garden of miniature plants in a laboratory bottle can have delicate beauty, yet require a minimum of care.

127

7: Wind a larger plant gently in a cylinder of paper in order to slip it through the bottle neck. This technique is effective for leafy plants like rex begonias, African violets, and some ferns.

8: With tongs, make hole in soil surface. Carefully and patiently manoeuvre roots into place. Add other plants, determine final positions, and shape the terrain. Cover all roots with soil, and firm soil.

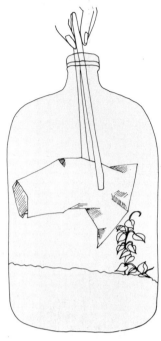

C

Figure C: Insert plant in its paper cone through bottle neck. Using tongs, shake paper to release plant inside. Remove the paper, and proceed as in photograph 8.

9: To water roots into place, use rubber syringe with an extension. This tool is also convenient for washing or blowing away soil particles that may adhere to the leaves and the bottle's inside wall.

10: With a single-edged razor blade taped to a stick of suitable length, prune unwanted growth inside bottle garden. Remove clippings and spent flowers with tongs or mechanic's pick-up tool.

BOTTLE GARDENS CRAFTNOTES

Light, temperature, and moisture in proper balance will keep your bottle garden growing. Bright daylight is ideal but avoid direct sun. Where there is no bright natural light, place a standard fluorescent fixture, with two 20 or 40 watt tubes, one "cool white" or "daylight" and one "warm white," directly over the bottle; keep lighted 14 to 16 hours daily. Water if plants show signs of wilting, leaf greens appear dull, or beads of moisture do not form on the inside of the bottle. Spray a half glass of water over the soil. If signs of dryness continue after 24 hours, spray on another half glass of water. Remove any yellowing or dead leaves and faded flowers. Fish them out with tongs or the mechanic's pick-up tool. To prune unwanted growth, use a single-edged razor blade taped to the end of a stick. Twice a year, water with a liquid house-plant fertilizer mixed at half the strength usually suggested for feeding container plants.

☐ With tongs, make a depression in the soil in a position corresponding to the one the plant occupied in the paper circle. Set the plant in place, and push soil over the roots. Add one plant at a time until all are placed and turned so the grouping is attractive. Tidy the terrain, and make sure all the roots are covered with soil.

☐ Fill the rubber syringe with tepid water, moisten soil surface slightly.

☐ Carpet the bare soil around the plants with pieces of moss.

☐ Add decorative accessories, such as stones, shells, weathered wood.

☐ When the planting is complete, use tongs and paper towels to clean the bottle. Remove bits of moss or soil with a mechanic's pick-up tool.

Greenery and Growing Things
Geology in a Lab-Bottle Garden

Our second project requires a bottle purchased at a laboratory-supply house. The planting techniques are the same as before. The selection of plants (see figure B, page 127) is different, and for geological interest we have layered the growing media in this order: pea gravel, charcoal, sand, and soil. (To keep layers from washing and sifting together, cut pieces of nylon stocking and sandwich between ingredients.) As a colour accent, you might conceal in the soil a vial of water holding a cut flower. Small bottle gardens make welcome gifts and require minimal care.

CRAFTNOTES ON ENLARGING PATTERNS

Throughout the volumes of The Family Creative Workshop, patterns are reproduced for you to copy. To make a pattern full size, follow the system described here for enlarging the grid imposed on the heart pattern.

The system is really very simple. The small grid in the book must be translated on to a grid with larger squares that you will make; the design (in this case, the heart) will be copied on to this larger grid. The size of the enlarged grid you make will depend on what the pattern is for. For example, for a cushion pattern the grid will have much smaller squares than will a grid for a tablecloth or a bedspread. A gauge is given with each pattern printed. Draw the squares of the large grid you prepare to the size given by this gauge.

Before you cut your pattern, be sure an allowance has been made for seams.

Above is the pattern of a heart as it might appear in these volumes. The grid placed over it is divided into small squares that actually measure 3 mm. All the patterns in the Creative Workshop use grids of this size. To double the size of the heart, transfer the pattern on to a grid whose squares are 6 mm in size.

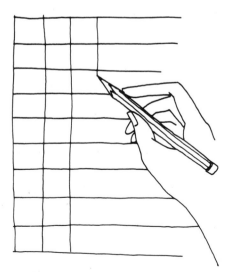

To enlarge the pattern, prepare a grid that has the same number of squares as the illustrated grid, but one in which each square measures 6 mm on each side.

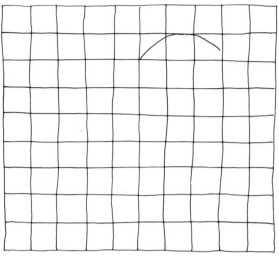

Draw pattern on to your 6 mm grid a square at a time.

Follow the lines around, checking the book as you go.

You will find it easy to transfer the whole pattern.

There is a craft activity that can transform odds and ends into beautiful and charming objects. The technique is called embedment, and it is done with polyester resin or, more expensively, acrylic plastic. In this form (and combined with other plastics), acrylic is a slow-moving liquid that pours like treacle. When another chemical, called a catalyst, is added to it, the soft plastic turns first to a stiff jelly and then into a rock-hard substance that remains crystal clear. Because of these unique properties, you can embed in a transparent block all sorts of objects. Although the plastic is poured in layers, one layer blends so perfectly with the next that you will not be able to discern the join. Use stock materials when you try plastic embedment, and keep notes on how they work, to find the brands that produce the results you like best. Don't mix different manufacturers' products: stick to one brand.

Tools

Strictly speaking, moulds are not tools. However, you will need them. To start, buy polyethylene moulds in a craft shop. These are made of soft, waxy plastic. Castings readily come loose from them. Experiment with ice-cube trays (the soft-plastic type) for small embedments such as rock samples or insects. Glass jars can be used only once, because you have to break them (gently) to release the casting. One small item that makes casting much easier is quite inexpensive, but you need a good supply—stirring sticks. You should have them in a series of sizes.

Measurements

Most proportions are determined by volume: millilitres or drops. For this, measuring cups and eyedroppers are fine. Later, as you get into larger work, you will probably find that it is handier to weigh the ingredients. Accuracy will demand that you use reasonably precise scales, but a good kitchen model will serve perfectly well.

Safety Precautions

Acrylic embedment is a reasonably safe craft activity, but don't be careless. If you are making large-scale castings and using huge amounts of liquid plastic, provide plenty of ventilation. In nice weather, work near an open window. Dust your workshop carefully before you begin work. Then set up a fan so that it moves a constant flow of fresh air through the work area. When you are making small embedments, no special precautions are needed.

Protect Sensitive Skin

If you tend to have allergic reactions, there's a chance you may get a rash from the chemicals used in this craft. Just a few precautions will help keep you free of such troubles. Wear rubber gloves when handling the liquid plastic. Be careful not to spill any of the chemicals on your skin. If you do spill a chemical, a quick wash with warm water and detergent should forestall any reaction.

Clean Work Area

Plan to do most of the casting on a sturdy table covered with several layers of newspaper. It is sound policy to mop the floor and vacuum dusty surfaces before you tackle any plastic-embedment project. Particles of debris drifting around in the air can settle into the wet plastic and become a permanent part of it; and this fluff rarely adds beauty to a project. For the same reason, develop the habit of covering the mould with a sheet of clear-plastic kitchen wrap while you are waiting for layers to harden. Clean moulds and measuring containers as soon as you have finished with them.

Casting The Plastic

Following instructions on the container, mix the exact quantities of casting plastic and catalyst needed for the first layer. In combination, these two will change the material from a thick liquid to a clear solid.
Add colouring agent and any other additives you wish. Stir well. Use a sort of cutting action to mix casting plastic and catalyst. The general idea is to combine them without introducing too many air bubbles into the mixture, which would weaken the cast.
Pour into mould to form the bottom or base layer of the plastic embedment.
Let set until plastic reaches the rubbery stage. Do not test it with your finger, because the fingerprint would remain and be embedded. Instead poke it with a wooden stirring stick. The plastic is ready when it is as firm as hardened gelatine and none of it sticks to the stirrer. Carefully place the objects to be embedded on the base layer, using tweezers if necessary.
Mix casting plastic and catalyst for next poured layer. Pay special attention to the instructions on the label, because the proportions of catalyst to plastic change with succeeding layers. As the stratification builds up, successive layers will absorb some heat from the lower segments, and this will make them gel more quickly. For this reason, multi-layered embedments are always cast in thin layers, which join without trace.
Continue mixing, pouring, embedding, and allow to set, according to the instructions for the plastic you are using.

Caring For Your Materials

Although the tools and materials required for plastic embedding are quite simple, it is important to take care of them if you want to use them for future projects. Treatment of moulds is critical. Do not use steel wool, scouring powder, or any similar type of harsh abrasive on them. Once you have destroyed its smooth surface, you will never again get a smooth casting from a mould. This warning applies especially to soft-polyethylene moulds, as these can be abraded with your fingernail. If they become scratched, toss them out and buy new ones.

Don't Embed Everything

It is easy to be carried away by this craft activity because it produces such interesting objects. But keep this fact in mind: not everything can be embedded. The basic list of objects that cannot be successfully embedded in plastic includes anything that contains water or is too close to being alive—undried flowers, fresh bugs, and fish, for instance, are difficult to work with.

Measure the exact quantity of liquid-plastic material needed for each layer poured. Proportions are critical. Follow instructions on plastic label.

Only small quantities of catalyst are needed to start the hardening action. Use an eyedropper here, but do it strictly by the book or the plastic won't harden.

A small casting will pop loose from the mould when the plastic has cooled. To test, tap it lightly with an orange stick. If plastic clicks, it is ready.

Using a medium-grade file and a very gentle touch, smooth off rough or uneven spots that may appear on the casting despite all precautions.

Sand the plastic after it has been filed to remove scratch marks. Use fine, abrasive paper placed grit side up on a flat surface. Sand lightly.

With a stitched flannel, buffing wheel, and plastic-buffing compound, restore surface sheen after smoothing the plastic. Begin with coarse; end with fine.

If the object you are embedding tends to curl away from the plastic, press it down lightly. Let base layer harden to gel stage before pouring next layer.

Coins sometimes cause the plastic to crack as it sets. To prevent this, pour in several thin layers of plastic, letting each gel before you pour the next.

Many items in the kitchen make excellent and inexpensive moulds. Easily identifiable above are such everyday objects as flexible ice-cube tray, jelly moulds, a tin can, soft plastic mixing bowls, and a ladle. Make sure moulds have wide openings.

METRIC CONVERSION CHART

EXACT CONVERSIONS: METRIC TO IMPERIAL

1 gramme=0.035 ounces
1 kilogramme=2.205 pounds
1 millimetre=0.039 inches
1 centimetre=0.394 inches

1 metre=1.094 yards
1 millilitre=0.035 fluid ounces
1 litre=1.76 pints
1 litre=0.22 gallons

OUNCES TO GRAMMES

oz	g	oz	g
$\frac{1}{2}$	14	7	198
$\frac{3}{4}$	21	8	226
1	28	9	255
$1\frac{1}{2}$	42	10	283
$1\frac{3}{4}$	50	11	311
2	56	12	340
3	85	13	368
4	113	14	396
5	141	15	425
6	170	16	453

POUNDS TO KILOGRAMMES

lb	kg	lb	kg
1	0.5	11	5.0
2	0.9	12	5.6
3	1.4	13	5.9
4	1.8	14	6.3
5	2.3	15	6.8
6	2.7	16	7.3
7	3.2	17	7.7
8	3.6	18	8.2
9	4.0	19	8.6
10	4.5	20	9.0

INCHES TO MILLIMETRES

in	mm
$\frac{1}{8}$	3
$\frac{1}{4}$	6
$\frac{3}{8}$	9
$\frac{1}{2}$	12
$\frac{5}{8}$	16
$\frac{3}{4}$	19
$\frac{7}{8}$	22
1	25
2	50
3	75

INCHES TO CENTIMETRES

in	cm	in	cm
1	2.5	11	28.0
2	5.0	12	30.5
3	7.5	13	33.0
4	10.0	14	35.5
5	12.5	15	38.0
6	15.0	16	40.5
7	18.0	17	43.0
8	20.5	18	46.0
9	23.0	19	48.5
10	25.5	20	51.0

YARDS TO METRES

yd	m
$\frac{1}{8}$	0.15
$\frac{1}{4}$	0.25
$\frac{3}{8}$	0.35
$\frac{1}{2}$	0.50
$\frac{5}{8}$	0.60
$\frac{3}{4}$	0.70
$\frac{7}{8}$	0.80
1	0.95
2	1.85
3	2.75

FLUID OUNCES TO MILLILITRES

fl oz	ml	fl oz	ml
1	28	11	312
2	57	12	341
3	85	13	369
4	114	14	398
5	142	15	426
6	171	16	454
7	200	17	483
8	227	18	511
9	256	19	540
10	284	20	568

PINTS TO LITRES

pt	lit
$\frac{1}{4}$	0.1
$\frac{1}{2}$	0.3
1	0.5
2	1.0
3	1.7
4	2.3
5	2.8
6	3.4
7	4.0
8	4.5

GALLONS TO LITRES

gall	lit
1	4.5
2	9.0
3	13.6
4	18.2
5	22.7
6	27.3
7	31.8
8	36.4
9	41.0
10	45.5

(All figures have been rounded off to simplify the tables.)